MW00861342

# BUILD YOUR SWING

"I've used Jim's ideas on the swing my entire life. His attention to detail is amazing and he teaches all levels of golfers with ease."

—Cristie Kerr, No. 1 ranked junior, No. 1 ranked amateur by age seventeen, No. 1 ranked player in the world in 2011, LPGA champion, twenty LPGA wins, U.S. Open champion. Cristie has worked with Jim since her teenage years.

"I have known Jim McLean for a long time, having competed against him in college and important amateur events and later on tour, and I can personally attest to his ability! His swing was admirable—long and solid. He became a fine teacher and a loyal servant to the game as a club professional. Anyone would benefit from his longtime advice about the game. Read this, seriously."

—Ben Crenshaw, two-time Masters Tournament champion

"Jim is super dedicated, super knowledgeable, and right at the top of his profession."

—Greg Norman, PGA Hall of Fame, two-time British Open champion, No. 1 ranked player in the world for multiple years

"Jim has taught me more than I could ever explain."

—Lexi Thompson, youngest winner on the LPGA Tour in history (age sixteen), No. 1 ranked junior and No. 1 ranked amateur at age fourteen. Youngest ever to achieve both rankings. Has qualified for six straight U.S. Opens since age twelve.

"Jim's teaching has helped with my golf swing over many years and helped to win the U.S. Open."

—Tom Kite, U.S. Open champion, twenty PGA TOUR wins, PGA Hall of Fame

"When Jim McLean and I were at the University of Houston together, and even after, he might have been the best ball striker I've ever seen."

—Bill Rogers, British Open champion, No. 1 ranked player in the world 1981, World Match Play champion, World Series of Golf champion, Grand Slam champion, college Player of the Year

"I never saw such an improvement in my game! Jim McLean is one of the biggest people to help my career."

—Keegan Bradley, PGA TOUR player,
winner 2011 PGA Championship in Atlanta, U.S.
Ryder Cup team, winner of the PGA Grand Slam of Golf

"I thank Jim McLean for believing in me and sharing his knowledge of the game with me."

—Gary Woodland, U.S. Open champion 2019, four-time
winner on the PGA TOUR, runner up WGC Match Play

"Jim McLean had the best golf swing I have ever seen. Jim helped me get back on tour after I took the ABC commentator role in 1992. He worked with me a ton. I came back to win and make the Ryder Cup team."

—Peter Jacobsen, U.S. Ryder Cup team,
nine-time PGA TOUR winner

"Jim McLean is an incredible teacher of the game of golf, and I am so lucky to work with him."

—Bo Hoag, qualified for the PGA TOUR 2020,
winner on the Korn Ferry tour

"Jim McLean has dedicated his life to the study of the real fundamentals that all great players have in common. He defined these corridors of success to help thousands of players ranging from major championship winners to amateur players of all levels. His latest book is a master class in a game improvement system that Jim successfully used to create the No. 1 ranked golf school in the country and an unmatched legacy of training countless top-100 teachers and outstanding PGA professionals. *Build Your Swing* is a must read for game improvement and a "must have" for every serious golfer's library."

—Jeff Warne, *GOLF Magazine* Top 100 Instructor,
cohost *Golf School* on SiriusXM with Jim McLean.
Director of Golf at The Bridge, Bridgehampton, New York.
More than twenty years with Jim, including assistant to
Jim at Sleepy Hollow Country Club, Briarcliff Manor, New York.

"I have always admired Jim's success as one of the great teachers of the game and especially his business acumen."

—Jerry Pate, U.S. Open champion, U.S. Amateur champion, TPC champion, U.S. Ryder Cup team, U.S. Walker Cup team

"I started my golf lessons with the Jim McLean Golf School when I was twelve. Jim has helped me with every part of my golf game. He is the best at making golfers better."

—Erik Compton, No.1 ranked junior, University of Georgia All American, runner-up in the U.S. Open, winner on the Web .com tour, U.S. Walker Cup team, ESPN Espy Award for Courage

"Jim McLean is a golf expert. He has been highly successful in every facet of golf—great teacher, author, businessman, player, head professional, and mentor. His passion and love for the game is contagious. He is a lifelong learner who has created a tremendous lasting impact on teachers and players around the globe. He is truly a legend in golf instruction."

—Justin Poynter, *Golf Range* Top 50 Instructor, U.S. Kids Top 50 Instructor, director of instruction at Jim McLean Golf Center, Jim McLean Junior Academy (year round), teacher to PGA TOUR members Carlos and Alvaro Ortiz

"I've never met anyone with as much dedication to the game, teaching, and mentoring others. Unlike other teachers, Jim teaches a system and not a strict method. He understands that everyone is built differently and there are a lot of different ways to swing a golf club. This is why Jim McLean has been successful with golfers at every level and has gained worldwide notoriety."

—Adam Kolloff, director of instruction, Jim McLean Golf School at Liberty National, Jersey City, New Jersey, teaching assistant to Jim for two years, owner of Pure Drive Academy in Boston, Massachusetts, top-ranked golf instructor

"I'm grateful every day to have Jim McLean as my mentor."

—Jason Carbone, Top 100 Teacher in America, director of instruction, Baltusrol Golf Club, Springfield, New Jersey, ten years with JMGS

"I am so proud and thankful for all the guidance and mentorship Jim has given me over the years."

—David Armitage, director of golf, La Gorce Country Club, Miami Beach, Florida, director of instruction, Queenwood Golf Club, London, England, top-ranked teacher in Europe and America, director of instruction, Jim McLean Golf School at Miami Beach Golf Course for five years

"Thanks very much to Jim McLean for all the training over many years. It was an incredible run for me. He had a great vision and led the way. He has a huge impact on thousands of people. Most of all, the guys that worked for him."

—Christopher Toulson, director of golf, Sunningdale Golf Club, Scarsdale, New York, top-ranked teacher in America, director of instruction, Jim McLean Golf School, more than twenty years at JMGS

"Jim has made an incredibly positive impact on me and so many other golf professionals. I am forever thankful for those simple rules he has instilled in me."

—Mario Guerra, director of golf, Quaker Ridge Golf Club, Scarsdale, New York, more than ten years teaching with JMGS

"Jim McLean has taught me so much as far as the game of golf, but just as important—how to manage and better motivate people. I note how well he treats those around him and takes a genuine interest in bringing out the best in all. All my friends and family, whom I have brought to his schools over the years, have commented on how thrilled they are to have improved their games because of him."

—William C. Kunkler, executive vice president, CC Industries Inc.

# JIM McLEAN

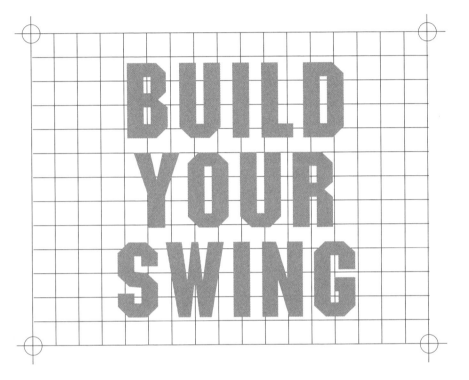

# BUILD YOUR SWING

Position Teaching in the Modern Age

## ILLUSTRATED BY PHIL FRANKÉ

RADIUS BOOK GROUP
NEW YORK

Distributed by Radius Book Group
A Division of Diversion Publishing Corp.
443 Park Avenue South, Suite 1004
New York, NY 10016
www.RadiusBookGroup.com

Copyright © 2020 by Jim McLean

All rights reserved, including the right to reproduce this book or portions thereof in any form whatsoever. No part of this publication may be reproduced or transmitted in any form or by any means, electronic or mechanical, including photocopying, recording, or any other information storage and retrieval, without the written permission of the author.

For more information, email info@radiusbookgroup.com.

First edition: May 2020
Hardcover ISBN: 978-1-63576-994-4
eBook ISBN: 978-1-63576-990-6

Library of Congress Control Number: 2020900786

Manufactured in the United States of America

10 9 8 7 6 5 4 3 2 1

Cover design and illustration by Phil Franké
Interior illustrations by Phil Franké
Interior design by Neuwirth & Associates Inc.

Radius Book Group and the Radius Book Group colophon are registered trademarks of Radius Book Group, a Division of Diversion Publishing Corp.

# CONTENTS

ix

x

# PRELUDE

I have run golf schools and major golf instruction programs for thirty years. Tens of thousands of students have come to Jim McLean Golf School (JMGS) for golf lessons and golf programs. They come from all walks of life: CEOs, plumbers, celebrities, artists, real estate moguls, teachers, engineers, salespeople, and doctors who have been successful themselves. In their fields of expertise, they have rules. They have also broken their profession skill sets into progressive steps. They have not done that in golf.

Instead most arrive confused about what to do and how to practice. Often their ideas are incorrect. They are trying to combine contradictory ideas or methods they have seen on TV, read in magazines, or discovered on social media. They listen to their friends who are teaching clichés. They arrive desperate. We know we have to get them on a new path. We slow these students down and approach teaching with fundamental positions in a step-by-step process. We get success every time. My teachers understand how to build a swing for students by using position teaching. I teach the fundamentals that are common to top ball-strikers. These fundamentals were derived through decades of meticulous research and then proven through the success of our students. My teachers are all trained diligently on using safety zones and tailoring specific golf movements, the steps

(S positions), to each student. It is imperative to impart the correct ideas, at the right time, to our clients. The key to running omit top golf school is having top trained professional teachers singing off the same sheet of music. Confusion kills golfers. Tension kills the golf swing. Bad positions kill tempo and rhythm.

In this book I tell you how to fix and improve the faults you might have in your golf swing.

I have been fortunate to teach major champions on the PGA, LPGA, and Champions tours. When these tour players talked about me in the press, I received national attention. While I've loved teaching the best players on the planet, my best teaching has probably been in developing young players and teaching the average golfer. Developing a golfer is much different than working with someone who is already on the tour.

That's mainly what this book is about. I tell you how you can develop a golf swing. Some golfers need more pull or lag in their swing, while others need more throw or release. I try to balance out each person I teach. They may need to get the shaft more vertical in the backswing, or maybe they need more depth in the backswing. They may need more restriction in the hip coil, or more turn. Every student is different. There is no one way, but there are steps to take for every golfer.

# BUILD YOUR SWING

## INTRODUCTION

# SHOW ME THE VIDEOTAPE

Great players will sometimes describe a feel that they are not actually doing. That's because a feel can fool you. Not only that, but feels change. Plus, the verbal description of a feel is illusive. I prefer the visual proof. My research partner Carl Welty taught me long ago, "Don't tell me what you do, show me the videotape." So, no matter who tells me something about the swing, or what some famous player says he or she is doing, I'll go to the tape and I'll analyze it.

When teachers start showing you pictures as proof of a move or position, it means nothing to me. Carl showed me the importance of correct positioning of the video camera. A picture taken from different angles or different heights changes everything when studying a golf swing. Without consistency, you cannot do proper research—and Carl was fanatical that we did our video work perfectly. We are in a time of science and analytics, so it's crazy not to think you can build good golf swing mechanics. Especially when we know the corridors and the safety zones.

An amateur golfer will naturally be ambiguous in describing a feel when they are asked to make a swing change. That's why my teachers must sometimes exaggerate a movement to get the student into the safety zones. There have been many times when I filmed a midhandicap golfer making a practice swing while trying to change a bad position, and they still could not make the change. At JMGS, we describe the really bad positions as "death moves." This serves three purposes: First, to shock the student into understanding they are in a very bad place. Second, no good player is ever in this position. And third, to show them what a death move looks like, so they can help make the corrections. If you have had a death move in your swing for a long time, it's called a habit. A habit feels natural and it takes a good deal of work to change. The good news is, we break bad golf-swing habits all the time. I teach a system that all teachers can use, and that every level of golfer can use to improve.

## DEATH MOVES

1. Freezing over the ball with no waggle and/or ignition movement.
2. Leaving the majority of your weight on your left leg on the backswing to such a degree that the left leg becomes the pivot point.
3. Overextending or "disconnecting" the left arm from the upper torso during the backswing.
4. Rolling your hands over dramatically in a clockwise direction during the takeaway.
5. Too little hip turn combined with no weight shift.
6. Turning the clubface into an extremely shut position during the backswing.
7. Turning the clubface into an extremely open position at the top of the backswing.
8. Right arm folding immediately into the body.
9. Allowing the clubshaft to tip forward in a steep orientation on the downswing.
10. Dropping the clubshaft under the right arm as you start the downswing.

11. The body sliding or drifting past the ball on the forward swing.
12. Dramatic lifting or dipping in the backswing.
13. Having weight on toes at setup.
14. Making a fast move away from the ball with the hands.
15. Allowing the head to move in front of the address position while hitting a driver off the tee.
16. Spinning the back foot at the start of the downswing and shifting the lower body away from the target.
17. Throwing the club from the top of the backswing with the hands without initiating the downswing with a lower-body shift.
18. Disconnecting the upper left arm from the left side of the chest, breaking down the most important body connection.
19. Letting the left wrist break down at impact.
20. Allowing the clubhead to travel inside out past impact with the club shaft vertical.

## EXPLAIN BUT VERIFY

Instruction without verification is poor instruction. Using video or visuals until a student does understand the difference in feel is always what I'm looking to achieve. We have detailed video research and other high-tech tools now at our disposal to prove clearly what positions are off. This book calls attention to the fact that much of what is still widely taught in golf is just simply wrong. It will show how modern teaching gets it right. As you probably already know, a majority of teachers will naturally teach what they do with *their own* golf swing. They will teach the same method day after day, no matter who the student is. I disagree with that type of teaching.

Instructors must teach the student in front of them and have many ways for students to improve ball-striking. Each student we work with has to leave us as a better golfer—that's a rule at JMGS.

## Research

When I started my Doral golf school in 1991, I had every teacher and assistant do a study on one aspect of the swing using data collected during the Doral PGA TOUR event, which was one of the richest events on the PGA TOUR. As a result, we were able to film virtually every top player in the world. We felt we needed a hundred players in the study. Back then the players didn't care about the filming, and it was easy to get the players filmed correctly. Many times they would go back to the camera to take a look at their swing. One year (around 2008) we were filming so much at the Doral event, the PGA TOUR staff actually banned us from videotaping. I even got a letter from a tour lawyer. This was the only tour event where they stopped allowing outside video. So we just videotaped at the other tour events. I have teachers everywhere.

Now we see about 80 percent of the golf galleries with smartphones videotaping the players, just as all fans are allowed to do at all pro-level sporting events. Those video clips won't show good angles for research, but it helps grow the game, and golfers enjoy watching the top professionals, no matter what the angle.

In recent years, I would sometimes have fifty or more teachers doing these detailed studies at different tour events. At Doral, I even played in the tournament. Plus, every year we had the inside-the-ropes views, making it easier to get great clips. For most years, my staff could record the swings of every player in the field. Some of the tour players would come down to my school at the end of the range to hit balls, take lessons, train, get filmed, or use our technology.

When I wrote *The X-Factor Swing*, almost every tour player used the Sports Motions Trainer to check their X-Factor numbers. Before my move to Doral, I taught for five years at Westchester Country Club in New York, where we hosted a PGA TOUR event—the Westchester PGA Classic. I played in the tournament twice. One time I had a practice round with Payne Stewart when he made an ace. Nobody was filming that shot! I was a one-man show in those days. Filming was always an all-day assignment in hopes that we got four or five really good clips. (That's because of the galleries and the difficulty in getting the perfect angles. If the angles were bad or if the player hit a bad shot, we threw out the clip.)

As the director of golf for six years at Sleepy Hollow Country Club, I helped host a Senior PGA TOUR event. I spent hundreds of hours with Lee Trevino, Gary Player, Peter Thompson, Al Geiberger, George Archer, and Bob Charles in my Superstation video room going over every golf-swing position. These great players loved it. At other Jim McLean Golf Schools, there also have been big-time PGA golf events, including one at Mayakoba in Mexico. I had a school at PGA West for seventeen years where they held the Humana PGA TOUR event. At my Texas Golf Center, we were thirty minutes from Colonial and thirty minutes to the Byron Nelson Classic. And at Liberty National Golf Club in New Jersey, we had the Presidents Cup and two FedEx Cup playoff events. I tried to attend every one of those events. So you can see the incredible access I've had to tour pros and the opportunities to film a huge variety of the greatest golf swings. After decades of research, we have a very good hold on the fundamental positions used by all the best players in the world.

Unlike most golf instruction, these fundamentals were not clichés or theories—they were indisputable principles. It comes down to this definition: "Truth is conformity with a fact or given reality." Every truth has a story, and I'll be using stories to illustrate key ways of learning the swing. In this book, you might gain a new way of learning how to improve your swing by the way a tour player benefited from a drill. Whatever your level of golf—from advanced to a weekend warrior to someone trying to break 80—these stories are meant to inspire your pursuit of ball-striking improvement. The best teaching often gets started with a story. So let's get started.

## Fundamentals

1. The golfer achieves center contact.
2. The golfer generates clubhead speed.
3. The hips do not stay on a level rotation in the backswing or forward swing.
4. For all great ball-strikers, the downswing arc is narrower than the backswing arc.
5. The golfer uses four main power sources: hands (wrists), arms, weight shift, and rotation.
6. The golfer executes a two-pivot-point swing, using the ground.
7. The golfer engages lateral motion.
8. The golfer's head moves in the golf swing.
9. When the golfer's hands get to waist height on the backswing, the right arm is even or above the left.
10. The golfer's shoulders out turn the hips in the backswing.
11. The golfer's hips change axis.
12. In transition, starting the downswing, the golfer's right elbow leads the right hand.
13. With the golfer's driver swing, the head is well behind the ball at impact.
14. The lead arm is connected or pressed against the upper part of the body at the armpit starting down to impact. This means the lead arm does not move independently away in the downswing, it has a connection to the armpit.

15. The golfer's shoulders, upper center, arms, and club rotate in unison past impact.
16. The golfer's left (or forward) wrist is flat or slightly bowed at impact.
17. The golfer's right heel (or back heel) leads the toe of the right foot at the start of the downswing.
18. The golfer's lead arm and the lead knee (left arm and left knee for the right-handed golfer) are forward of their address positions at impact.
19. The golfer's upper center of the body is more forward at impact on all iron shots than it was at address (setup).
20. At impact, the golfer's hips are more open to the target than the shoulders.
21. Everything at address (setup) is different at impact.
22. The upper body tilts somewhat toward the ball target line at the finish.
23. The golfer's right shoulder passes under the lowest point of the left shoulder in the backswing.
24. The weight/pressure is transferring forward before the golfer completes the top of the backswing.
25. In the change of direction, the golfer's clubhead stays inside (or behind) the hand path. The shaft plane should not be too steep or outside the hand path. All top ball-strikers have the clubhead behind the hands at Step 5a.

## OUTLINE OF THE BUILDING BLOCKS

At JMGS, we put a teaching plan together through steps. That's how I am going to teach you a top-class golf swing in this book. Here's a summary of the building blocks. It's still basically "The Eight Steps" from my earlier writing, with the addition of the four positions used by the instructors at my golf schools. These steps are explained in detail throughout the book.

### Section 1

**Step 1a.** We start with setup. I use a "pro example" for each stage of the swing, or each building block. You may read about my work with well-known professionals, or how I have closely observed tour professionals working on a key position. You will also see the illustrations for every important building block. It is critical that you see the alignments. Think alignment golf.

**Step 1b.** This is the first "in-swing" move—or what Ben Hogan call the first crossroad of the swing. I show you an ignition move to start your swing and numerous ways to get your golf swing moving off the ball correctly. Jack Nicklaus called this "the most important part of his swing." Jack serves as the pro example for this important step.

## Section 2

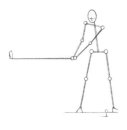

**Step 2.** The halfway-back position has to be learned and mastered. This is the position that almost all teachers agree upon, although I might surprise you with the clubface alignment. I show you how to sync the body and the club to this important checkpoint step, and exactly what details to check.

## Section 3

**Step 3.** So many amateurs go wrong at the three quarter back position when they allow the club to get too flat and too far around. I'll teach how to balance the golf club, and how to know if the clubface is in a strong position.

## Section 4

**Step 4.** What are the things we need to achieve at the top of the backswing? I'll show you how to improve a weak position and make it powerful. You can create a powerful X-Factor. This is why I'm often called a golf-movement teacher. I'll show you when the backswing stops and when transition begins.

## Section 5

**Step 5a.** This building block takes time and effort to master. It's not as easy as the other positions, but learning it will change everything for your ball-striking. We learn to use the ground for added power. We learn powerful wrist positions you must achieve. You will understand why I call this the moment of truth. It's a huge piece of my original X-Factor writing.

**Step 5b.** This is the biggest discovery Carl Welty and I made in breaking down the golf swing. It literally took decades. Carl and I labeled it the "on-line delivery plane." It's the first part of "the powerline."

## Section 6

**Step 6.** Impact has been called the moment of truth, but the moment of truth really happened earlier at Step 5a and Step 5b. I want you in a great impact position with the hands forward and with your body in the correct angles. Knowing is not enough. I will show you how to get there.

BUILD YOUR SWING

**Step 7a.** We keep things moving in sync past impact, but many students do not. They tend to hit *at* the golf ball and not *through* the ball. Their body stops, and their arms fold up. A good golf swing should feel as if there was no ball to hit. I like my students to feel that the center of their swing is three feet past the ball.

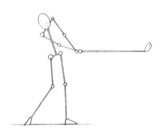

**Step 7b.** My staff and I always work hard at extension position, because it's such a key building block with our students. Poor extension is almost always a result of previous mistakes. However, by moving students into the correct extension position, their swing often dramatically overcomes the mistakes.

**Step 7c.** This position is best checked from down the line. I focus on the exit plane of your shaft. Although this is a position that I've checked for decades, it is still relatively new in today's teaching. There is a safety zone from the top of the lead shoulder to the middle of the back, so you have a wide area. But outside this safety zone is

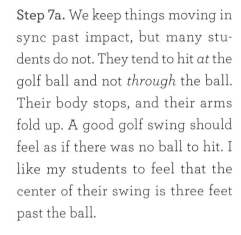

11

the death position. I'm also looking at your spine tilt and the angle of your shoulders in relation to the shaft's exit after impact. Carl and I basically invented exit plane, and I wrote an article about this for *Golf Illustrated* all the way back in 1989.

**Section 8**

Step 8. The finish of your swing is a good indicator of balance and freedom. Many golfers cannot hold their finish, while others never complete the finish due to tension in the arms and hands. At JMGS, we teach the pro finish relentlessly to our students. I use Rory McIlroy as the perfect pro example for the classic pro finish.

## TIMING, TEMPO, AND RHYTHM

The product of a strong and powerful golf swing is the way we observe it. The power and accuracy of a top golf swing looks almost effortless. PGA TOUR players make golf look like an easy sport. As a teacher, I have heard this all my life: "How do they achieve that kind of distance?" The answer is they have the body and the club in great position, and they make a world-class transition into the forward swing. They have worked hard on the principles of an athletic golf swing. I always work on flow with my students. Good positions allow you the chance to amass huge power and really look good when you swing a golf club. You have the ability to "let go!"

We will work on body action:

1. Weight shift (side to side or horizontal)
2. Rotation (turn)
3. Vertical (using ground force to press down and up)

At the same time, we'll work on the club:

1. The arc of the clubhead from inside the target line.
2. The shaft moves on one plane going back and another plane on the way down.
3. The plane of the shaft rises and lowers throughout the swing.

# SECTION 1

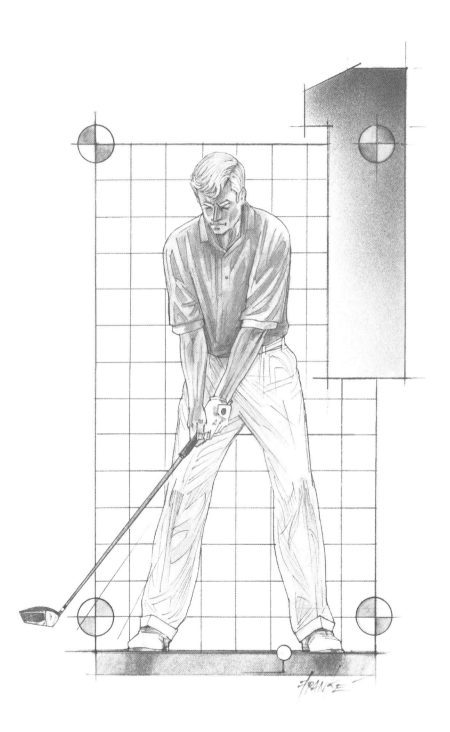

# THE SETUP

I'm using what I'll call "pro examples" in this book to teach you how I've communicated with and taught the best, and what I've learned from close observation of top tour players. The Phil Franké illustrations are another way you can assimilate ideas on how to improve your golf swing. The combination of stories, examples, great illustrations and vivid teaching concepts taught in a step-by-step manner will allow you to diagnose and address issues in your swing you may not have known existed.

## Pro Example: Tiger Woods

There are a few classic tour models I've used to teach my students a good setup, and a great place to start is Tiger Woods and his perfect address position. But let's drop back in time to see how his setup really developed. Tiger's first teaching pro was Rudy Duran, when Tiger was five. Rudy happened to be a fine golfer with the enthusiasm to give his time to a young golfer. They played golf together often at the 18-hole, par 3 Heartwell Golf Course in Long Beach, California.

Tiger came to Duran after first learning how to swing from his father, Earl. Both Rudy and Earl had good golf swings. The elder Woods used photographs of Sam Snead's swing as the model to teach his son. In fact, Earl called his son "Sam" around the house. (Interestingly, Tiger later named his daughter Sam.)

You couldn't have a better model to learn a great golf swing from than Sam Snead. I definitely give Earl Woods huge credit on teaching those Snead alignments and swing characteristics to his young son. No one should ever underrate the early lessons from Mr. Woods.

When Tiger was eleven, Earl hired the best teacher in Southern California—John Anselmo—who taught only fifteen miles away from the Woods' home in Cypress. John was well known and had a long list of successful players at that time. He's the one who really molded the Tiger Woods swing through the important developmental period when all children have the gift to imitate.

There is a time that all children have an incredible ability to copy. That ends at about age seventeen, though not completely. So the time Tiger spent with John Anselmo is underrated. If you have the interest, read John Anselmo's book, *"A-Game" Golf*, and you will see how his teaching style dealt in vivid imagination skills and in making his teaching fun. You'll get an idea of what great junior teaching is all about. You'll also probably note why so many tour players were first taught by their fathers, and that those fathers had great golf skills too.

When Tiger turned seventeen, Earl Woods contacted Butch Harmon about teaching his son, and my friend Butch accepted. To me, there is nobody better than Butch. Like Earl, he also had a military background and the two connected—and so did Butch and Tiger. It was a perfect fit.

Butch and I have done numerous golf schools together and many PGA educational seminars. We're both fundamental teachers who grew up in the game. Butch's father, Claude, was a Masters champion and the longtime pro at Winged Foot Golf Club in Mamaroneck, New York. (I was at nearby Westchester Country Club at the start of my teaching career). Butch grew up

TIGER

50 50

A great set up
position to copy.

in a golf family and his father, Claude, was someone I spent
many hours talking to about golf, including the smallest details.
Later, I would take many lessons from Claude at Morningside
Country Club when I took the winter director of golf position at
Tamarisk in Rancho Mirage, California. With Claude Harmon
right across the street and Ken Venturi often at Morningside,
too, it was an incredible time to learn from the masters of the
game. By the way, both were best friends with Ben Hogan, and
you could always see the respect they had had for Hogan.

I also grew up in a golf family and lived next to a golf course. My father, John, was a Boeing engineer and a lifetime golfer. He was a structural engineer who helped build the tail sections of the 757, 767, and 777 airplanes in the Seattle area. We lived right next to Boeing Field, although the 777 was mostly built in Everett, Washington. He qualified for three U.S. Senior Amateurs once he slowed down on his job. My dad worked forty-four years for Boeing and won numerous club championships.

Butch Harmon refined and perfected Tiger's setup, especially the setup for his wedges. Tiger Woods does have perfect body position and alignment, and I love for my young students to copy every aspect of it. (And they enjoy hearing Tiger Woods stories.)

I had a two-hour meeting in my office with Earl Woods in the early 1990s. Earl was in Miami, and he called me about a meeting. He came down to my Doral office, and I believe he was interviewing teachers for his son. Tiger played in the Orange Bowl each year, held at the famous Biltmore Hotel. (He won it twice).

Here are a few highlights of our meeting that Miami afternoon: Earl told me that Tiger would do far more than just play golf. He would break every one of Jack Nicklaus's records, and he would win more than twenty majors. He told me Tiger's short game was already better than anyone on the PGA TOUR. He told me people focused on his length, but it was his mind that separated Tiger from all the rest. Golf was not going to be the only thing that Tiger would do in life. He told me his son would be the most recognizable person on the planet, and that Tiger would do something far beyond just playing golf. Earl Woods sat on the edge of my desk and had a forward look as he spoke. There is no doubt in my mind that he believed every word. I've always known how important it is for someone to believe in you 100 percent. Tiger had that with Earl Woods.

## THE SETUP

There are so many nuances to teaching the setup properly, but small fundamentals are crucial to your success. Pay attention to the details and it will pay off. The correct address position is crucial to making a good golf swing—it's the starting point, and the setup predetermines many in-swing mistakes. I'll emphasize all the things you need for an effective setup position, and alert you to common mistakes I see on the lesson tee—poor stance, alignment, grip, etc. If those things are off, what chance do you have of making a powerful and accurate swing? I think we all know the answer—zero.

Anybody can easily look at the top players in golf, past or present, and see their swings are not the same. You don't even need a slow-motion replay to see it. So why do so many instructors teach a rigid method? I think mostly because it's easy. When I traveled to meet top teachers, take lessons from them, and study their teaching methods, I was often surprised at the confidence some had in certain positions as an absolute. As I compared methods, it was obvious that some players did well with one approach to golf instruction and others did not.

The problem was that golfers who could not adapt to a teacher's method would not improve. Sometimes they even got worse. I thought I could help many more golfers by widening the corridors—or what I started terming "safety zones." There is some latitude for the positions you need to be in, particularly if it suits your individual preferences. If I can get you stay within these safety zones, your ball-striking will improve. One of the hallmarks of this book, and good golf instruction in general, is that it preserves the good things you already do when you swing and corrects the areas that contribute to bad shots. If you're in a position outside one of these corridors, your swing will suffer. I've termed being outside a zone a "death position."

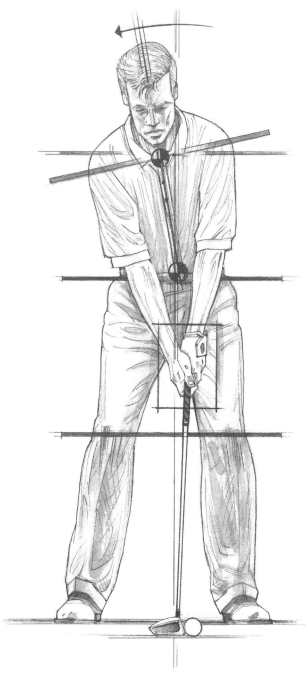

Spine tilt for the driver is 9 to 12 degrees away from the target.
Notice that the upper center is behind the lower center (represented
by the dots).

**BUILD YOUR SWING**

So stay inside the safety zones, and you're on the way to perfecting your swing.

Lexi Thompson at setup. I always tried to get her in a comfortable position with perfect alignments.

## SETUP STEP 1A

I call this the universal fundamental, because top teachers agree on its importance. My staff at the JMGS have learned how to teach setup through the experience of successfully helping thousands of golfers. We stress key elements that anyone can learn. I teach my instructors *alignment golf*, which begins with the clubface. The first procedure is aligning the clubface and clubshaft for the shot you intend to play. It's vital for our students to form the stance around the club—never the other way around.

In building your stance, there are *three balance points* during the swing. I teach these carefully to my students. The first balance point is a setup. Think of two triangles as you assume the address position.

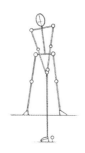

1. Setup
2. Inside of trail leg
3. Finish on top of lead leg

The upper triangle is formed by the shoulders and torso and sits on top of the lower triangle. The lower triangle is formed with your two legs and belt, or center of mass. To get in a good setup, center your core directly between the hip girdles and balance yourself with 50 percent of your weight supported by each foot. You can check that you're properly balanced by bouncing each foot up and down, moving pressure side to side and back and forth. Imagine you are standing on two separate scales to feel perfect balance. This establishes the first of the three balance points.

The two triangles at setup: the shoulders and arms form the top triangle. Draw a line from each shoe to your belt. This forms the lower triangle. Stack the upper triangle on top of the lower one.

1. Your body is balanced at setup. (We could say "centered.")
2. In the backswing, you will be balanced over your trail leg.
3. At impact and into finish, you will be balanced on your front or lead leg.

Once you can sense these basics, you can adjust balance (or weight) at setup for all types of shot requirements. *The feet are key to gaining balance, establishing balance, and moving in balance.*

## Adjustments

Weight distribution and shoulder angles change at setup depending on the shot requirements. For example, the driver setup is different than your setup for an iron shot in the fairway or a bunker shot. With the driver, you're standing on a flat surface and the ball is teed up. This means you need to hit slightly on the upswing to get the best distance. With the exception of a putting stroke, the driver swing is the only one where the desired angle of attack is ascending. On all other shots, the required angle is downward.

Now that you know this, here are the balance-point and shoulder-angle recommendations for the driver: Visualize a three-lane highway down the fairway. If your ball flight is right to left aim to the right lane. Your draw will put you in the center lane. A straight drive will keep you in the right lane, in the fairway. A hook can still catch the left lane.

Play the ball near the heel of the lead foot.

Distribute your weight so a little more than half (up to 60 percent) is favoring your trail foot. Tilt your spine slightly away from the target. (I'm always careful not to have my students lean too far away: 9 to 12 degrees is in the safety zone.) Position your

head so your lead ear (left for right-handers) is three inches farther away from the target than the ball.

Lexi Thompson, illustrated here in a JMGS Superstation.

Check that your shoulders are angled so the lead shoulder is
higher than the trail shoulder. Set your legs so they also are angled. The lead leg should be angled roughly 7 degrees away from
the target. This means the foot is outside the hip, which is extremely important. The trail leg (right) is angled more (9 to 11
degrees), away from the target. The farther you place the lead
foot forward, the easier it will be to get lateral motion forward in
transition. I'm always checking the position of that lead foot. It
must not be directly under the lead hip.

The iron setup is different than when using a driver, since
your goal with an iron is to strike down on the ball. To do this
the ball moves back in your stance. I've noticed that most iron
shots are played off a line straight down from the left ear.

3° TILT →

45%

55%

## Setup Checklist

1. Your look is symmetrical.
2. There are no unnecessary angles.
3. Weight is balanced between the feet.
4. Weight is centered near the ball of each foot, slightly favoring the heels.
5. The grip is adjusted according to your shot shape.
6. The head position is level and the chin is up off the chest.
7. You can draw a straight line from the tailbone to a point between the shoulder blades.
8. The head, upper spine, and neck (cervical) tilts forward about 20 degrees from the spot opposite of the center point between the top of your shoulder blades.
9. The arms hang soft, not rigid or tight.
10. The knees are slightly cocked inward. You can sense the inward pressure in the legs.
11. The muscles on the inner portion of the thighs are activated.
12. You have a clear mental picture of the shot you are hitting.

## Heavyset Pro Model (Craig Stadler)

If you're a big-chested man, a good pro to copy is Craig Stadler. In his case, pay close attention to the lead arm. I show students how they must get the lead arm on top of the left pectoral (chest) muscle at setup. A person with a large chest must not place the left arm to the side of the body. Craig also employs a hand press as his last move before starting the swing—like an ignition switch. He looks very relaxed and ready to go at address.

# STADLER

Craig Stadler: the setup for a big body.

**THE SETUP**

## Heavyset Amateur Model (Sly Stallone)

I taught Sylvester Stallone for many years and he became a fine golfer. It was during the days not long after the movie *Rocky*, and Sly was the No. 1 Hollywood star. Everywhere I went with him, people would yell "Yo, Rocky." He had two bodyguards at all times, but I can tell you when it came to golf instruction, he was totally tuned in. Actually all actors are good at focus. Actors have been some of my easiest students.

Sly had the habit of putting his left arm on the side of his body. Since his chest was so massive, placing the left arm over the breast wasn't comfortable. I noticed he had to go around his chest with his left arm, so I thought about just moving the left arm on top of the chest. I've taught this alignment ever since. If you're big-chested guy, I know it's the same for you.

We fixed the problem with a setup trick. I had Sly place both arms and the club straight out with the arms squeezed slightly inward. From there, I had him drop the club down to the address position.

Wow, what a difference in his takeaway. All of a sudden, he could wind the arms, shoulders, and hips in sync. He took away the loop he had at the beginning of his swing, and his golf improved dramatically!

## Pro Example: Cristie Kerr

My pro model for female golfers is Cristie Kerr. She sets up beautifully. Cristie and I worked on her setup for decades. In fact, whenever I see her now, she'll ask me, "How does my setup look?" Cristie doesn't miss a thing. It's one reason why she's America's all-time leading money winner on the LPGA Tour and a two-time major winner, including the U.S. Open.

Notoriety for a teacher comes from teaching the pros. Most

people want to hear about how I teach Cristie Kerr, Liselotte Neumann, Lauri Merten, Jane Geddes—all U.S. Open champions—or Lexi Thompson, who is a U.S. Junior champion and Kraft Nabisco (now ANA Inspiration) champion. The truth is, I teach all these golfers the basics, the same basics. I've taught major champions on the LPGA Tour and many professionals winners, but I've also taught many state, junior, amateur, and men's and women's state champions.

*Cristie has always been extremely diligent with her setup alignments.*

At JMGS, we teach a great setup position, all part of alignment golf. At address, the head should feel comfortable, not rigid or stiff, and the golfer is looking through the center of the eyes. I get down low to watch how the eyes work.

## FALLACIES IN THE SETUP

Regardless of the instructor's intention, sometimes the instruction explaining how to get into the perfect setup simply aren't true. When that happens, you're wasting your time and not improving your ability to hit the correct shots. Here are five things that are routinely stated about the setup that are wrong:

**You should always set up parallel to the target line.** FALSE. It's great for practice and for most golf shots, but it's not a fundamental. Remember these setup facts: Nicklaus set up open; McIlroy sometimes sets up closed for driving.

**You should keep your back straight.** FALSE. The top section of your back and neck lean (tilt) forward.

**You should try to re-create your setup position at impact.** FALSE, not even close.

**You should start with your hands positioned closer to the target than the ball.** FALSE. This is not always true. It depends on ball position and the type of shot your trying to hit. For example, a bunker shot of normal length would be played with the hands farther away from the target than the ball. Most tour players set the hands behind the ball with a driver.

**You should address the ball in the same position no matter what club you're using.** FALSE. This idea is preposterous. Ball position greatly impacts trajectory and shot shape and should always be taken into consideration before swinging. The ball is played forward with a driver to aid in hitting it on the upswing. The ball is played farther back with short irons to ensure crisp contact.

Here is more description of killer setup positions. If you find yourself in a poor setup position, you're destroying your chance for a quality shot before you even take the club back.

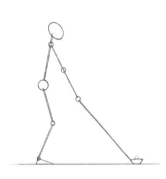 

Wrong—The straight line back. Still taught by some. Very rigid. A line down from the hip pockets would strike the heels. Avoid this mistake.

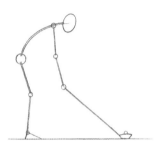 

The rolled back. No. This the lazy man's position with the chin buried into the chest making it impossible to coil properly.

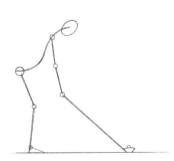 

The sway (S) back. This position puts the head too far forward. The hip pockets are more than six inches outside the heels. I usually see inward extension coming into impact. Causes back problems. Avoid.

**THE SETUP**

## BALL POSITION

The idea of playing the ball in one position for all shots is horribly flawed. Just think of all the variables in any given golf shot—lie angles, wind conditions, slopes, etc. You form a new stance for each shot you hit. The only stance that can be considered the same, day in and day out, is your driver stance. Why? You're almost always hitting off a flat piece of turf and can choose the tee height. Ball position also can remain absolutely consistent.

Here are the basic ball positions depending on club selection. For short irons, play the ball roughly centered between your feet. For a driver, however, play the ball in line with the heel of the lead foot.

Here is an illustration showing ball placement:

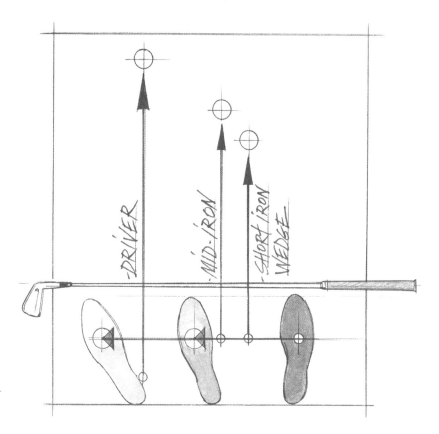

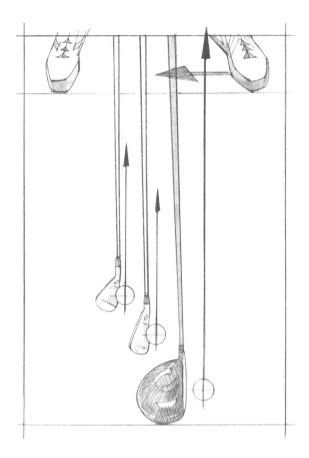

**Mistake.** Golfer's body is too far ahead of the ball. This fault can occur either with the upper torso or head. It will be excessive if the golfer makes a lateral slide toward the target.

The effect of getting ahead of the ball before you strike is most often an open clubface (see Steps 2, 3, and 4). This leads to an early release of the club (known as casting). By impact, the golfer is in a poor impact position—causing high, weak shots. To fix this error, often a golfer moves the body forward and past the power position. You can still hit serviceable shots making these two mistakes, but you'll never hit it great.

## Pro Example: Ken Venturi

I teach ball position the way the U.S. Open champion Ken Venturi taught me. I started working with Ken when I first came to New York in 1975 (my first teaching position at Westchester Country Club). We had a great team at Westchester that included PGA TOUR Hall of Famer Harry Cooper (thirty-six PGA TOUR wins) and LPGA great Mary Lena Faulk (who was taught by Harvey Penick). My education was in high gear, and I loved learning new things about the golf swing. Every part of the game intrigued me. One of my students, Francis Santangelo, introduced me to his friend Ken Venturi. Ken stayed with Franny during the Westchester Classic (now the Northern Trust), one of the PGA TOUR's top events. Ken was then the lead analyst with CBS Sports (something he ended up doing for thirty-five years). His mentors were a couple of gentleman you might have heard of— Byron Nelson and Ben Hogan. *The Match*, one of the best golf book ever written, was about the famous match between two then amateurs—Harvie Ward and Venturi—against golfing legends Hogan and Nelson. Ken Venturi was a virtuoso of golf and had an incredibly sharp mind on technique. He could strike a golf ball with magical control. He taught many of golf's greats, such as Tom Watson, John Cook, and Tom Weiskopf.

I could not get enough golf information from Ken, and I asked him questions for thirty years. We played about a hundred rounds together, and he always came to see me at the courses in New York where I was the head pro. When I moved to Doral in Miami, we had a PGA TOUR event every year, and CBS did the broadcast for most of them, so I got to see my friend even more. Venturi taught me on every aspect of the swing, and it started with how to get into a good setup. He told me "most golf shots are missed before the club is taken away." He advised to keep the hips tucked inward and the core engaged. Ken taught me incredible ideas about the setup and I present many of them here. When it comes to ball position, Venturi passed on to me something Hogan told him. Ben Hogan said to find your ball position using the lead foot (his left foot). Here's how:

## Ball Position

Start with your feet together and the ball centered. Then take an alignment stick or golf shaft and place it between your feet.

Keegan Bradley showing a centered ball position with an 8 iron.

**THE SETUP**

Then sidestep toward the target with your lead foot and do the same away from the target with your trail foot. Note that the ball is now in the center of your stance. Use the lead foot to get exact ball position every time.

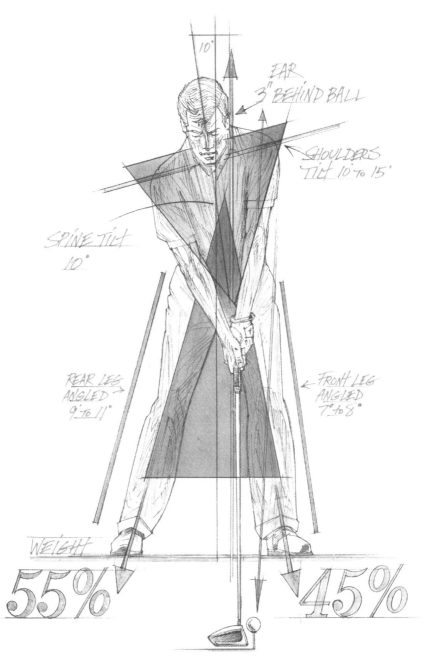

Note on ball position: you change ball position depending on the circumstance. Downhill, the ball should be played back of center in your stance. When swinging short irons, the ball is centered. When chipping, the ball is centered or sometimes addressed slightly back of center.

And as I mentioned earlier, when driving the ball, it should be played forward—in line with the heel of the front foot is the most common spot. You build a stance for every shot you hit. You stand balanced at the correct distance from the ball and with the correct ball position. You can learn to do this just like the tour pros.

## Driver Ball Position

With your feet together, flare your left toe out somewhere from 10 to 30 degrees. Then take a big lateral step away from the target with your trail foot. This puts the ball correctly off the inside of your lead heel (left for right-handers). The ball position can be adjusted, albeit slightly, depending on your preference. Some golfers like the ball slightly back of this position. Lexi Thompson is a good example. Some like it farther forward than the heel. Tiger is now playing the ball more forward in part due to his back surgeries and to help his angle of attack. He drove it great in winning the 2019 Masters (his fifteenth major). But no matter where you address it, always use the lead foot to find the right ball position.

Get into the correct position with these moves:

Sole the clubhead, adjusting its face for specialty shots (open, closed, etc.). The club's shaft will be oriented differently depending on ball position. For example, the shaft will noticeably lean away from the target if you take a wider stance or play the ball way forward.

39

1. Aim the club face.
2. Step laterally toward the target with the lead foot.
3. Step laterally away from the target with the trail foot.

Turn the toes outward to increase hip rotation. Many top ball-strikers set the toes on the trail foot perpendicular to the target line to help brace that leg and restrict hip turn during the backswing. This allows the more flexible golfer to turn the hips freely. A braced trail knee is your governor to stop overrotating the hips, which can be a power killer. Meanwhile, the toes of the lead leg are flared to help improve hip rotation during the forward swing. These adjustments are a matter of personal preference. Jack Nicklaus and Lee Trevino turned their left foot out 45 degrees. Others, such as Jordan Spieth, keep that foot relatively perpendicular to the target. This explains why Spieth's left foot rolls to the target side as he completes his swing.

## DISTANCE TO THE BALL

How far should you stand in relation to the ball? There is no one set distance, because your golf clubs have different lengths and lie angles and these changes your distance from the ball.

Common instruction dictates that the club should be held one hand-width from the body. That's good basic teaching, but upon closer inspection we've found that the distance varies between great players. But one fundamental holds true: if your hands are too far away from the body, your weight moves too much into the toes of your feet. This also disconnects the lead arm from the shoulder. Having your hands too far away is a mistake. That lead-arm connection is vital.

Too much distance leads to bad shots. You never see better players address the ball with the hands too far away from the body. In fact, you'll often see them with their hands nearly touch-

40

ing the body. (Too close is definitely better than too far.) Greg Norman addresses the ball with his hands very close to his body, and he was No. 1 in the World Golf Ranking longer than any other player except for Tiger Woods.

Here are my recommendations for hand positions:

**Wedges:** Keep your hands close to your body to promote a more vertical swing and better accuracy.

**Driver:** Keep your hands about six to eight inches away from your body to accommodate its length and flatter swing plane, and so you can hit the ball on the upswing.

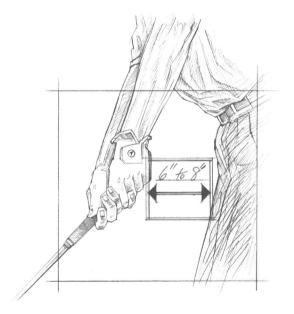

There are no absolutes on the distance golfers hold the club in relation to the ball, because of the limitless variances on players' heights, weights, length of arms, size of hands, ages, spine tilts, etc. But the thing I ask myself is, do the hand positions promote contact on the center of the face? If they don't, it's time to make adjustments.

It's been interesting watching Bryson DeChambeau progress into one of the best players in golf using most of his clubs at one length. This idea of one length for all clubs has been tried before, but not with the success Bryson's had. This again goes to my overall point in teaching the game of golf. There are many ways to play! Bryson also uses super thick grips which helps take out hand action. Bryson is a huge Ben Hogan fan, and Hogan used oversized grips himself. I'm sure that didn't get past Bryson. (More on Bryson on page 212.)

## THE GRIP (CONNECTION 1)

There are two special connections in golf: your feet to the ground and your hands to the club. The purpose of your grip is to con-sistently square the clubface at impact. That's probably one great reason why all professional grips are not the same. So again, we have corridors to work with and adjustments to make with cer-tain students depending upon the size, length of fingers, strength, and how well they square the clubface. We adjust depending on the player. You form your stance around the club—not the other way around (a common mistake).

Holding the club correctly is more about your arm positions than most students would ever believe, and that aspect is not often taught. Start by bringing your arms out in front of your chest with the elbows slightly bent. Your palms should face com-fortably toward the ground. The arms are inwardly extended. All of this matters at impact.

Do not hold your hands palms up as if you were holding folders of paper.

*Do not put your hands on a club with the palms facing upward.*

Now bring your hands together with the left thumb fitting into the pocket of your right hand (left-handers should do the opposite). Once they're together, shut your fingers—this forms a beautiful golf grip.

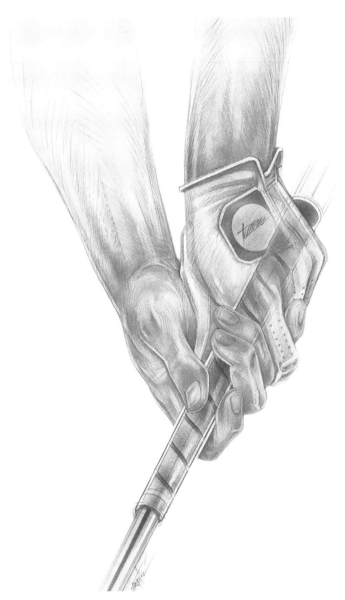

The forefinger is in a pistol position, separated from the middle finger. There is very little pressure in the thumb.

I suggest connecting the hands by overlapping the right pinky on top of the left forefinger.

This is called the Vardon Grip, named after the great Harry Vardon, who popularized this way of holding the club in the early 1900s. Most top players use this grip. You also can interlock the right pinky and the left forefinger—known as the interlocking grip. Several great players hold the club this way, including Jack Nicklaus, Tiger Woods, Nancy Lopez, Bruce Lietzke, Jordan Spieth, and Rory McIlroy. Another great, and one of my former students, Lexi Thompson, also interlocks.

## Grip Points

We have students grip and regrip the club numerous times. Most of the time we find they grip too tight. Then we move to other adjustments, such as turning the lead hand (left for righties) more palm down, which exposes three or four knuckles when you look down at address. This is a strong grip that promotes hooking, but it also tends to increase lag. For golfers with no lag, I'll often switch them to this stronger grip. Many top players employ a strong grip on the PGA TOUR.

Meanwhile, turning the lead hand toward the target, where you might see only one knuckle on at address, is called a weak grip. This grip encourages a fade or slice. It also can cause an early release. However, many current great ball-strikers employ a weak top-hand grip, including Justin Thomas. Remember, the purpose of your grip is to return the clubface to square at impact. The hands are simply your connection to the club. I focus on how a golfer holds the club with the lead hand, because it's on top and therefore has the most leverage. I call it the controller hand.

## Grip Pressure

Once I have your arms in the correct position and your grip looks good, I explain grip pressure and pressure points. When I began teaching the grip, it was difficult to express how light or tight to hold the club. It also was hard to show where the pressure should be felt in the hands, so I came up with a pressure scale. The first national golf magazine I wrote for, *Golf Illustrated*, published my 1-to-10 grip-pressure scale. I still use it in every school. The lowest number represents your lightest possible grip pressure. I teach students to hold the club with a 1 on the scale. Then grip it increasingly tighter, one number at a time. Five should feel like medium grip pressure and 10 should feel like you're squeezing the club super hard. I'd have students move all the way up the scale and then back on down to 1.

You can try it right now. Hold a club vertically (this is a balanced position and the club should feel almost weightless). If you rotate the shaft to the side, you will begin to feel the club get heavier. When the club shaft gets horizontal to the ground, it will feel quite heavy. This is because weight is at the end of a fulcrum, and gravity is pulling it downward. This simple exercise is an eye-opener for many students.

## Pressure Points

While working on grip pressure, I also ask students to feel the pressure in specific spots on their hands. This is key. The location of the pressure matters in terms of being able to make a good swing.

You should feel slightly more pressure in three spots on your hands:

1. The back three fingers of the left hand.
2. The middle two fingers of the right hand.
3. The connection between the left thumb and the lifeline of your right hand.

So sense these spots as you repeat the 1-to-10 scale.

Note: your right thumb should be very light on the club, never tight. To test this, push down on the right thumb and notice that it immediately activates the top tendon of that arm, encouraging coming over-the-top when you swing (bad move).

Repeat the 1-to-10 scale with your eyes closed.

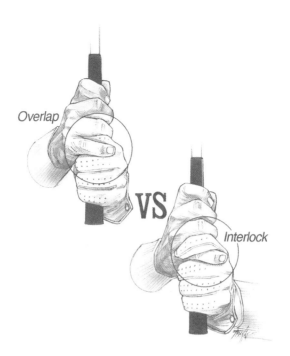

Overlap

VS

Interlock

## Pro Example: Sam Snead

Sam Snead once said golfers should hold the club as if they were holding a bird. Sam was an outdoorsman. He grew up in a rural area in West Virginia. To him, picking up a bird was somewhat common. Most of us do not hold birds and never have, so I'm not sure how applicable that advice is to you in terms of grip pressure. I've heard many other similes to grip pressure, like holding a tube of toothpaste and not letting the gel come out—not really great advice. Years ago, I spent three days with Sam producing an instructional DVD, and we discussed grip pressure in detail. Sam said it was something he checked every single day. He checked the orientation of the hands and the pressure points constantly. Sam knew slight changes could result in significant problems.

Getting back to the pressure points, feeling the club in the back three fingers of the left hand allows you to set the clubshaft on plane and control the face at impact. If you're feeling it there, you'll have the most leverage and security. This doesn't mean I want you to hold the club as tightly as you can with those three fingers. Remember to use the 1-to-10 scale, and if you feel like you're holding it around a 5, that's good grip pressure. If it feels like an 8, 9, or 10, it's probably too tight.

As I said, the second pressure point is in the middle two fingers of the right hand. There is very little pressure in the forefinger or thumb. I often tell my students to lighten up on the thumb. Jack Nicklaus said you could cut off his right thumb for golf, because he applied no pressure with it. And Ben Hogan correctly stated that pushing down with the right thumb activates the tendons on top of the right arm in the wrong place, causing the right arm to move outward and encouraging a mishit. That said, the thumb and forefinger form a trigger position similar to holding a pistol.

And the third pressure point? Hogan once said the connection between the two hands, where the left thumb sits perfectly into the pocket (or lifeline) of the right hand, should lock together like a jigsaw puzzle. I always liked that description, as it forms such a perfect picture for students.

In three days of recording video at Sam's home and then staying with him at the Masters, I got incredible time with one of the golf greatest players. His idea on checking his grip every day was enlightening, because I'm sure most golfers don't do this.

Sam said when he was off with his game, he would return home to the Cascades and take his shag bag of eighty balls down to a small range. He brought with him only his 7-iron. Sam said he never had to hit that shag bag more than three times before he had his timing back and his golf swing corrected.

There's a great lesson. Return to a comfortable place. Slow your tempo down. Hit your favorite club.

Sam liked to pick up his own balls too. He liked to see the pattern of his shots, and he thought pitching or chipping his shots back to the practice bay also was very good for his timing.

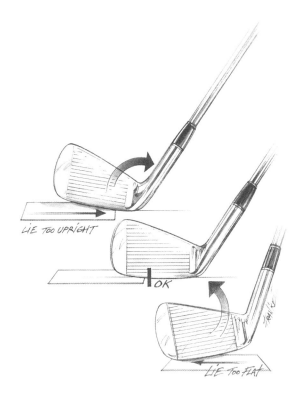

Check the lie angles of each of your irons.

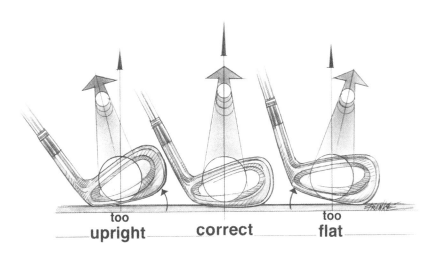

An upright lie will cause you to pull. A flat lie, with the toe, up will cause you to push. The flat lie with your long irons is particularly destructive.

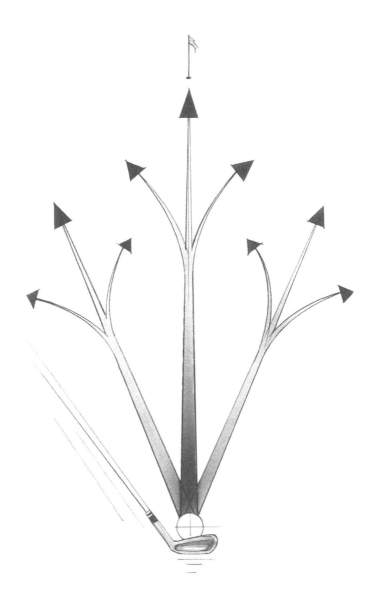

The PGA used to teach that the ball flight started on swing path and then curved according to the club face. Incorrect. The ball direction starts closer to face angle up to 90 percent with a driver, 70 percent with an iron. The lesson has been changed in recent times.

### Drill

Hold the club in the ready position, which is parallel to the ground. From there, it's very easy to see the angle of the clubface and the forward lean of the shaft. It's also easy to do a grip-pressure check and to observe the orientation of each hand.

With the arms set properly and grip pressure in the 4 or 5 range on my scale, you're prepared for the stance.

To achieve great golf posture, I have my students put the golf club down. I've used body drills throughout my career as part of what I call "The Elimination Theory." So put the golf club down from time to time to organize the body. Without the club, I work hard on balancing the student and taking out angles. Without the club the student can understand and feel the body structure much easier.

## STEP 1A SIDE VIEW

Looking down the target line, I'm checking the angles and alignments. I check the eyes, the shoulders, hips, knees, and feet. I'm looking to see if the golfer's alignment lines are parallel to the target line.

Note: since the trail hand (right for right-handers) is farther from your center than the left, the shoulders can be slightly open at setup—but only a few degrees. As I look from down the target line, I want to see one leg and one arm. I will see just a piece of the left hand, and the forearms should be level.

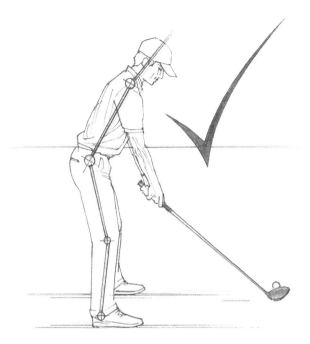

Good posture.

Rory McIlroy at set up with a 3 wood. Notice the space between the hands and body. The arms do not hang down straight.

*One of the great golf instruction images. The body sets on the inner rail. The club is on the outer rail. Think parallel lines.*

Notice the flexion of the knees. If you drew a line down from the knees, it should run into the middle of the foot. An average golfer often will have too much knee flex.

## Balance Drill

It's quite easy to determine weight distribution from toe to heel. Start by setting your body weight back into your heels. I want you to feel this as a reminder that it's a poor position to be in when you swing. Conversely, if you shift your weight into your toes by leaning forward, you're also in a bad position to hit good golf shots. Practice moving your weight forward and backward, so you develop a keen sense of how your weight should feel centered in the feet—not in the heels or toes. The weight should be evenly distributed between the balls of each foot, perhaps slightly toward the heels.

Your clubs are graduated in length, so the distance between the clubhead and your body will vary. The short irons are held in a more upright position and will be the closest to your body.

Your hands will be the farthest from your body when holding a driver. As I mentioned earlier, the idea of keeping your hands one hand-width away from the body is only an approximation and is certainly not how many great players address the ball. I have seen and taught many great golfers who've had the hands in close to the body for iron play. Like I said, too many amateurs incorrectly reach out for the ball at setup.

## Note on Setup lines

A top teacher will adjust setup lines for a student's ability level, often to help with the swing plane. Stance lines vary for sidehill lies and for intentional hooks or slices. On the practice tee, I recommend adjusting your shoulders and hips, not simply the feet. Once you start swinging on plane, you can slowly work your way back to a more conventional stance.

# IGNITION

The first move in your takeaway might make no sense: it's actually *toward* the target! This slight move forward sets the body into motion and is something the golfer can rebound from. I call it a "micromove." You could say it's the ignition move to starting the golf swing prior to the bigger move called the back-swing. The micromove is often imperceptible to the eye, because it might be just a slight move of the hips or a slight shift of the body. Other times, this move is easy to notice. The purpose of the ignition is to help the golfer go from a motionless start to a fluid, athletic takeaway. The ignition move helps many golfers swing the club smoothly away from the ball and in sync with the body. Some great players, like Ernie Els and Sergio Garcia, use a hand press toward the target as their micromove. It's very easy to see, and it's definitely used by many top-class putters.

### Pro Example: Jack Nicklaus

The most common pro ignition is a slight weight shift into the lead side (left side for right- handers). The player then rebounds off this micromove by starting his or her backswing.

Other ignitions might be a push of the hands or a small kick-in move of the trail knee toward the target. While many use this weight-shift ignition move, there are exceptions. Jack Nicklaus

57

started his swing by turning his chin away from the target and firming his arms. I'll use other examples of Jack at takeaway, but let's focus on eye dominance, because it can make so much difference in your head rotation or head movement. Others have used a pivot of the chin to start the swing, but I caution you that Jack Nicklaus is left-eye dominant. So was Ben Hogan. So is Tiger Woods. It's fairly uncommon to be a right-handed golfer with left-eye dominance. The right-handed golfer who is left-eye dominant will have the advantage of being able to turn more and not lose sight of the ball. Many right-eye dominant golfers have more lateral head motion in the backswing, so they can keep that eye on the ball. Left-eye dominant players cock the head away from the target.

A right-handed, right-eye dominant golfer will slide the head in the backswing, or they will lose sight of the ball.

## KEY POINTS TO REMEMBER ON THE IGNITION MOVEMENT

Many teachers disregard the importance of a forward ignition move (or some other type of move to get the swing started fluidly), but I don't. It's one key part of having rhythm, tempo, and timing in the golf swing. Almost every golfer needs some kind of move to get the swing started correctly time after time.

### The Waggle

The waggle is a preparatory move that is usually combined with the ignition movement. Its purpose is to relieve tension and rehearse what is about to take place. It should only be a small motion with the hands and arms with minimum use of the body. Think of it as a small golf swing above the ball with the hands and arms simulating what will happen once the actual swing begins. A common waggle is to lift the clubhead from behind the golf ball, then push the club over the ball, and then cock the club behind the ball. It's an up-over-and-back motion.

My goal in teaching a waggle is to get you to take the tension out of your elbows and loosen the wrist joints. There is no one way to waggle. If you observe golf's greatest players, you'll see many different styles. But no matter how it looks, the intent is always to get the golfer in the right frame of mind to take the club back. I encourage all my students to develop relaxing pre-paratory movements even if they are very small (the micro-move).

The three moves of the golf swing:

1. Micro is toward the target.
2. The minimove is into the backswing coil.
3. The major move is back to impact and into the finish.

## TRUTH: THE HEAD MOVES IN THE GOLF SWING

Harvey Penick said, "Show me a golfer who does not move their head, and I'll show you a golfer who cannot play." Considered one of the greatest teachers of all time, Harvey Penick had an undeniably great record with students. Any teacher who has seriously studied the professional game knows the head moves, yet many continue to believe that keeping the head still is a fundamental in golf. In truth, it's a swing-killer. Harvey knew this a hundred years ago. Anyone who read *The X-Factor Swing* saw the data twenty years ago. All biomechanics experts know it now. Why do golfers still hang on to the notion that the head should stay still?

I want to clarify what I mean by head movement in the backswing, because it's dramatically different depending on the length of the club being swung. Understanding the difference will alleviate a lot of confusion as it relates to head movement.

The head moves where the body takes it. Though the amount it moves is small, it should move.

## Head Movement from Step 1a to Step 7a

In our detailed swing studies of head movement, all tour pros moved the head in a full swing in some direction, which could be up or down, side to side, or out and back. We measured head movement from setup to just past impact, monitoring motion horizontally and vertically. Bubba Watson, interestingly, had the most recorded movement, at 17½ inches. The average head movement of a top-100 player in our studies was more than ten inches, more than almost anyone would believe (and in all directions). I'm very doubtful that any other school has come close to the detailed studies done by my teachers and JMGS. Bubba Watson, by the way, has been one of the top ball-strikers on the PGA TOUR. He is undeniably one of golf's greatest drivers. Joe Compitello, once my personal assistant and now one of the top-rated young teachers in America and the director of golf at the famous Indian Creek Golf Club in Miami, did this superdetailed study on head movement.

## Head Movement with a Driver

From setup with the driver, the head can rotate away from the target, move laterally away from the target—or both. Starting forward, the head responds to the lateral slide of the lead knee.

Because the driver is swung from a flat piece of ground but the ball is on a tee, the requirements of impact change. The angle of attack is more horizontal, or slightly ascending for maximum distance. Knowing this, the head should never go ahead of the address position. In fact, the head should have a recoil action. All top drivers move their head behind their address position when they strike the ball, but the same doesn't apply to iron shots. Very few golfers know this, but it can really help your ball-striking tremendously. You'll have different head movement when swinging a driver compared to a short iron

The head obviously moves in a full golf swing. The chin has its own swing, mirroring the club. Your head does not stay frozen in place, causing tension, back problems, and weak golf.

Why does the head move away from the target during a driver swing?

1. The ball is played in the front part of a player's stance.
2. The width of your stance exaggerates the ball's forward position.
3. The two setup adjustments create a natural tilt in your shoulders, setting the trail shoulder below the lead. (The driver setup will create the most tilt away from the target.)

**IGNITION**

4. The correct movements of the body allow you to coil and load correctly during the backswing.

5. The correct sequence of motion in transition goes like this: the lower body leads while the shoulders and arms complete the finish.

6. Starting down, the trail leg creates downward pressure. Notice how the spine is now tilted farther away from the target—what we call a second axis tilt. In fact, the amount your spine tilts away from the target will double from its orientation at address.

## Home Practice

To practice correct ball and body positions, use a mirror. Then make slow swings stopping at key steps. I'd suggest fifty practice swings done in slow motion. You will learn so much about correct movements and how to make the changes in your swing. If you can't afford that much time, do five slow-motion swings. I'll settle for that, and it only takes one minute.

## BODY MOVEMENTS AND BODY ANGLES

I'm showing you the back cover of my *X-Factor* book. This clearly reveals that the core (your belt) moves forward while the shoulders and arms are still going back. This "two-way move" forms an increased gap created by the disassociation of the shoulders and pelvis. For example, if your shoulders turn 90 degrees in the backswing, but your hips turn 50, the X-Factor gap is 40 degrees. In transition, the hips lead the forward swing while the shoulders stay back momentarily, and this increases the X-Factor gap. In this example, say 10 degrees more.

That stretch gives your lower body the lead required to make a more powerful golf swing and has increased your differential

This illustration copies the back cover of *The X-Factor Swing* (1997). There is so much to study. Notice how the hips start first while the upper body is still turning away. This is "stretching the X," a key move for all top golfers.

to 50 degrees. Modern biomechanists use this picture to reveal even more sophisticated data that has proven the X-Factor concept. I used data collected in 1992 with the Sports Motion Trainer developed by Michael McTeigue in California. Later, I hired biomechanics expert Dr. Rob Neal to work for me at my teaching headquarters at Doral using the GBD Biodynamics golf swing analysis machines (2003–14). The most important idea to practice and incorporate into your swing is, the shoulders follow the hips at the start of the downswing. If a golfer starts down with the shoulders first, the stretch is lost, and proper sequencing is ruined. You will read more about this in the transition Steps 5a and 5b. Please note how the right foot and leg push downward in the *X-Factor* drawing. This is how you effectively use the ground for more power.

Warning: an inactive lower body in the downswing is the main culprit for poor head positioning with the driver.

## HEAD MOVEMENT WITH AN IRON

When great ball-strikers transition into the downswing, you can see a large majority of them lowering their head as they move toward impact. Because the goal with irons is to strike down on the ball, the head should move slightly down and forward, not back and away. It can't be a coincidence that the greatest iron players all lower their heads from setup. Many golfers would have thought this was a terrible mistake, which again proves how golf theory of the past is wrong in many instances. Were you taught golf fundamentals that were just not true?

The head moves downward due to the flexing of the knees and the application of pressure into the ground with the feet. During transition with an iron, a player's weight quickly shifts to the lead foot. By impact, the weight should be 80 to 90 percent on the lead foot. As weight and pressure shift toward the target, the chest moves more on top of the golf ball. Ken Venturi described this forward move to me many times when we played or talked golf. I told Ken that he looked like he fell into his left side. He absolutely agreed and said this was one of the great things Hogan did in his swing. Venturi told me he just tried to copy that move. I described this fall into the lead-side knee in the book *The Complete Hogan*. I like the thought, *fall forward*, and I've used it so many times in teaching better golfers. Pros move down and slightly forward. That's mainly how the magic happens.

This is a fundamental move for great iron play and gives a player greater ability to compress the golf ball. It also moves the low point of the swing ahead of the ball. With an iron, this low point is three, four, or even as much as five inches ahead of the ball. It's the correct use of your body that makes this impact condition happen.

To teach this, I first show golfers the swing or photos of a tour player of their choice, noting how that player's head moves. Then I demonstrate why this happens. Next, I have the student rehearse swings in slow motion. As the proper execution of the desired movement improves, the golfer can start swinging faster. Finally, I have them hit shots. Anyone can master this move, which will allow the club to travel on a much better angle of attack.

## Pro Example: Gary Player

Ben Hogan called the takeaway the first crossroad in the golf swing. Ken Venturi beat this into my head during the years we worked together, and I've taught this section of the swing to every student. It's a very underappreciated part of the swing.

I'm using an all-time great for my example of how a pro starts the club back correctly—Gary Player, winner of nine major championships. When I was the director of golf at Sleepy Hollow in

Scarborough on the Hudson, New York, we had a PGA TOUR Champions tournament for all six years. It was so great to have legends of the game visit with me. Quite a few of them came down to my teaching center for lessons or to check their golf swings. It was site of my first "Superstation," and I had tons of fantastic videotape. Al Geiberger came down often. So did Jim Dent, Dana Quigley, Bob Charles, Gibby Gilbert, and many others who wanted to see the videos or get videotaped themselves. It was nonstop visits all week.

Nobody seemed to love the facility more than Gary Player. Gary and I had long discussions about the golf swing, and he asked to have his swing put on video and to get my opinion of it. But what Gary wanted to talk about the most was a videotape I had of Ben

GARY PLAYER
TAKE-AWAY

**BUILD YOUR SWING**

I always check the trail arm movement. The elbow should not attach to the body. I look for the space appearing between the elbow and the body. Some students like the idea of a floating trail arm.

Hogan's swing. We would look at it for hours. One year he came down after shooting a 74 in the opening round of the tournament. We watched the Hogan clips over and over, especially one swing Gary had me play back continually. Since I had videotaped Gary, I showed him his takeaway compared to Hogan's. We immediately went to the range and worked on his backswing. On the range, Gary told me that he had always tried to copy Hogan's take-away. He loved every part of Ben's swing and knew it all started with that move to begin the backswing. Gary wanted everything to start together like Ben's swing and realized that he had been neglecting this part of his swing. He saw on the video that Hogan was standing wider, and that Hogan had kept the right arm higher. I worked on that move with Gary for about forty-five minutes until he announced that he "had it." The next day, he shot a 66 and came back to the teaching facility to tell me how important that first move was to his good ball-striking that day.

I learned so much from talking with Gary and listening to his Hogan observations. It was a great opportunity to be at Sleepy Hollow in those years and so important to my education as a teacher.

## TEACHING THE GOLF MOVES

Many of my students have commented that I teach golf moves. I think that's true, as I move them from position to position trying to get a bit of improvement each time.

To get a student into a better position, I first show them what it should look like (picture or demonstration). Then I explain what I want them to do. I again show pictures or video of a professional in the correct position (validation). Next comes having the student move into the new position (execution). After some work on correcting mistakes, the student then practices this move over and over until he or she gets it right (repetition).

Spending two full days with legendary basketball coach John Wooden in the early 1990s really solidified my belief in teaching the golf swing by focusing on positions. In fact, the step-by-step process above was inspired by Wooden, a master teacher who was perhaps America's greatest coach of all time. He walked me through this system of teaching and how he used it with his players.

## Wrist Setting: Takeaway Options

There are three basic ways to set the wrists in the backswing. The wrist setting will take place early, at waist height, or later near shoulder height. Each wrist set has advantages.

The wrists will naturally set earlier when you're swinging shorter and more upright golf clubs. There have been many top golfers who have employed an early set with all clubs. Several well-known teachers instruct this method, but it's just one way. Be aware that the early set can lead to a few swing issues:

1. The tendency to get too fast off the ball
2. The tendency to swing the hands and arms away from the body
3. The tendency to reverse pivot

Most top players use a random set, a term from Homer Kelley's *The Golfing Machine*. He described a natural setting of the wrists. Most top ball-strikers use a random set. The weight of the club, combined with suppleness of the hands, prompts the wrists to set naturally, without conscious movement to reach the half-way-back position (Step 2).

The third setting action is called a late set. You see this from long-drive competitors and tour pros who excel off the tee. This setting action is more natural with your longer and flatter clubs.

You see a wide takeaway with the wrist set occurring past Step 3. Examples of late setters are Colin Montgomery, Jack Nicklaus, Adam Scott, Justin Thomas, and Tiger Woods.

In addition, some top players increase the wrist set starting down. This is called "downcocking" (increasing the wrist set in the downswing).

## The Drag Set (Teaching Lag)

Many golfers and teachers are surprised when I show them video of great ball-strikers who take the club back by letting it drag behind the hands. The hands move before the clubhead does.

The purpose of this move is not widely understood. Ken Venturi used a drag takeaway, and so did his mentors, Ben Hogan and Byron Nelson. This move is still effective today. In fact, here's a list of current top ball-strikers who employ the "drag-lag" takeaway: Paul Casey, Sergio Garcia, Angel Cabrera, Jason Dufner, Bubba Watson, and Justin Thomas.

They're following in the footsteps of other great players who dragged it: Venturi, Nicklaus and Greg Norman.

I use this takeaway to teach players how the club should lag behind the body's rotation in the downswing. Venturi called this type of action the "paintbrush swing," and I highly recommend this drill. You can even use it when you start your swing.

Starting away with center. There is no effort to wrist set. Instead the clubhead lags slightly.

**BUILD YOUR SWING**

The drag set. The hands have started the club away with the clubhead leaving last. The club slightly lags.

**IGNITION**

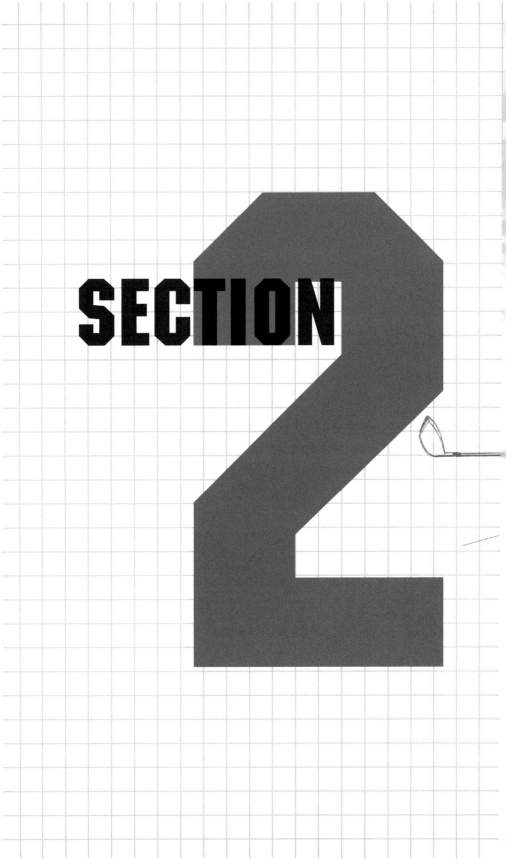

SECTION

2

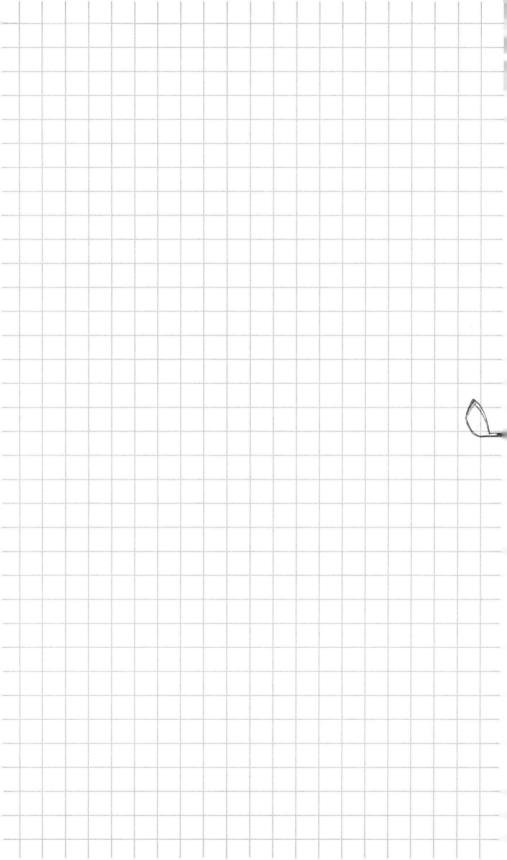

## STEP 2

# HALFWAY BACK

O f all the positions in this book, Step 2 is the one that has been taught for the longest period of time. I would say it has been taught for five hundred years, since the dawn of golf. It's a great spot to stop your swing and check it. What should you be looking for? First, understand that the Step 2 position is the farthest the club should ever be away from the target. All great swings work from being wide on the backswing to narrowing on the downswing—that's a golf fundamental.

The safety zone for Step 2 is the most generous. If you draw a line on the shaft at address, and then check the path of the club-head back to Step 2, there is no universal position among the great ball-strikers. Nearly an equal number are above the plane and below the initial starting shaft angle; therefore, I use a fairly wide safety zone. But I still carefully check the alignment of the lead arm and the clubshaft, so they are similar.

I also look for a good coil and sometimes the idea of the golfer "swinging the clubhead back to step 2." I hate to see a stiff or manufactured takeaway.

Below is the safety zone:

My preference is to have the clubhead and hands in sync when you're halfway back. I use the thought of handing the club head back to an imaginary baseball catcher in his squat stance. The shaft would ideally point parallel to the target line. It's interesting to check the orientation of the clubface, too, as there are contradicting ideas within the teaching community about how it should look. The oldest idea is that the toe of the club should be up. That's wrong! Nearly all top players in the world have the clubface toe-down at this point. It might only be slightly toe down.

As you take the club away, a good idea is to keep the clubface pointing at the ball. You must avoid the death move of rolling the arms and hands in the move away from the ball and having the clubface looking skyward.

**HALFWAY BACK**

Lay an alignment rod off your back toe, parallel to the target line.

The toe of the clubface should face slightly toe down or even parallel to the spine tilt. Some top ball-strikers have the clubface even more facing the ground. What really matters is that you should never have the face rolled over (open). That's a death position that my teachers and I will recognize and fix immediately.

Keegan Bradley at Step 2. Hitting an iron shot, the wrists have partially *cocked*. The lower body is resisting, but notice the shoulders and ribcage are coiling already.

## A POWER TAKE BACK

When I'm working with golfers who need more power or hit a lot of slices, I often change their Step 2 position. I make it a lot stronger. It's a magic move for many golfers. Since they typically have a weak wrist position at the top of the swing, that's the first thing I look to fix. When they swing to halfway back, I do two things:

1. Get the clubhead slightly behind the hands.
2. Bow the lead wrist.

This gets the clubface in a much stronger position early in the swing and automatically improves the position at the top of the backswing. The key is to get in this strong position at Step 2. I don't try to change things later in the swing—first things first!

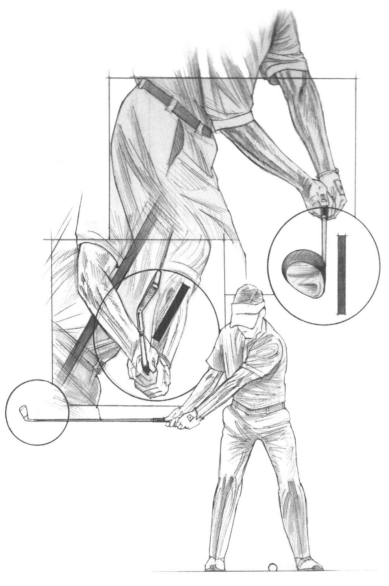

The toe of the clubface is in a safety zone from the toe up to very toe down position. No tour player rolls the face open at Step 2.

*Jim McLean staple drill.*

From Step 1 to Step 2, I usually see some setting of the wrists. If you keep the hands down and get the club head upward, the wrists will set automatically. I don't like to see the arms lift to Step 2. Remember: hands down, arms down at Step 2.

From the face-on view, the right arm is visible above the left. Also, check grip pressure. Be careful not to increase tension on the handle. Research has shown that most amateurs double the amount of grip pressure from address to halfway back. This added pressure is a mistake that will lead to a restricted, poor swing. Be very aware of this change in pressure. Maintain your address grip-pressure number from my scale, and you will get better ball-striking.

**Weight/pressure shift.** As the club and arms move away from the target in full swings, so should your weight. Feel that pressure moves into the right foot, right leg, or right thigh. As the club moves away so does the weight.

**The right arm.** The idea of a floating right arm is a great image for many of my students. The right arm must be free going away. You don't pin it to the side of your body. That's a killer move to Step 2.

The right leg is the backswing brace. You can see Lexi is already loading.

**BUILD YOUR SWING**

## KNEE ACTION

**Right knee.** The right knee is the "governor of hip slide and over-rotation of the hips." The idea of a floating knee works as an image for frozen knees, which is a violation of the X-Factor. There should be motion in the trail knee in a full golf swing. The right knee can even straighten slightly, but I do not teach a locking right knee. This usually causes the entire right side to lift excessively. Remember, zero movement of the trail knee is a mistake.

**Left knee and left foot.** You should feel pressure off the left instep, and the left knee will begin to move inward at Step 2. In my schools, I put a shaft on the ground between the students' feet and have them monitor the left-knee movement. On the backswing, the knee moves both inward and outward, pointing behind the ball.

**Spine and hips.** It's very important to not reverse-pivot. For many golfers I have them sense a slight slide of the spine and hips away from the target. It's so easy to turn only the hips, which leads to a reverse-pivot. I've heard many teachers teach the idea of a centered pivot, but then they say there is just a slight move. This would always come from a modern biomechanics teacher, because biomechanics will show the movement. Do the top ball-strikers move away? The answer is yes. I teach in reality. Others deal in theory. The hips do not turn in a perfect circle. So if you were looking at a backswing from the face-on view (chest facing you), the left hip should not move toward the target. Check this carefully when making swings in the mirror or watching on video.

## COMMON MISTAKES AT STEP 2

1. No hip turn, dead legs and feet.
2. Reverse weight shift toward the target.

3. Rolling the clubface open.
4. Locking the right knee and straightening the right side (usually because of too much hip rotation at this stage of the swing).
5. Overextension of the arms.
6. The right elbow folding into the body, restricting width.

## REVERSE PIVOT OBSERVATIONS AND RESEARCH

A big mistake is made by teachers who film from behind the golfer to observe hip action. The hips are connected by a hip girdle. Starting way back in the 1970s Carl Welty and I filmed from behind the tour players as well as from face-on and down the line. I am well aware of what the golf swing looks like from different positions. You get a very different perspective from behind the golfer and can easily get the wrong idea on weight shift and pressure shift.

There is a certain group of method teachers who believe the lower part of the spine shifts toward the target in the backswing. I could not disagree more. We have seen many golfers come to our schools after getting lessons from teachers using a reverse pivot mantra—usually from teachers working out of a shopping mall. When you read the pro example on Keegan Bradley (page 118) you will learn that the main fundamental change I made with him was eliminating the reverse pivot of the hips. Always check your pivot motion from face-on. Use a mirror or camera to watch how your lower center (your belt or belly button) moves. Use a center line, like a shaft on the ground, and watch to see that the belt moves "away from the target" and never toward the target. I like to see the belt move away and slightly toward your trail heel. The belt should move approximately two to five inches away. It's easy for you to visually check in a mirror.

## STEP 2 DRILLS

First, place an alignment rod parallel to your target line. The rod should touch the widest part of your right foot and be located on your toe line.

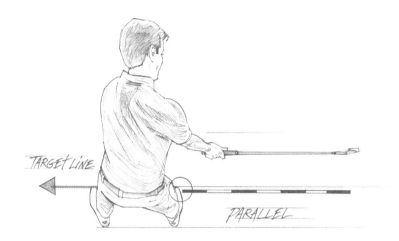

The classic takeaway, parallel to the target line at Step 2. You can use an alignment rod on the range to work on the takeaway. The clubface is turned slightly toe down.

Practice taking the club away to Step 2, and then check to see if your club's shaft lines up with the rod on the ground. Repeat over and over until your shaft and alignment rod are parallel virtually every time. This is a great halfway-back position

Next, get into your address posture and then move the right arm and hand to the halfway-back position. It should have the look like you're about to shake hands with someone. Now move the left arm and hand until they connect with the right. You'll notice that the left hand must move down and turn toward the right foot. If you overextend the right hand, you won't be able to connect with the left. Remember that the right elbow should begin to fold with an iron swing. In a driver swing, many greats keep the right arm long to create more width (power).

Then, watch your swing in a mirror as if you're swinging away from it. Check your body angles. Look to see if the club covers your hands as you take it back. You shouldn't be able to see your hands in the mirror. This is what I want you to check as you rehearse backswings over and over. Keep doing this until you're comfortable taking it to the range. Become an expert at them and your ball-striking will improve.

## THE BACKSWING MISCONCEPTIONS

Take the clubhead straight off the ball in your takeaway. FALSE. The clubhead ideally should work up and slightly inward on the swing-plane arc.

Keep your weight on your lead leg in the backswing. FALSE. A classic reverse-pivot.

On a full golf swing there is a centered turn. FALSE. Only with the small swings will there be a centered turn. There is always a small move away or a loading movement in a professional swing. For long shots and metal woods, employ a two-pivot-point swing.

On the takeaway, the shaft stays between the arms and shoulders, and the hips (you could say pelvis or the core) begin to coil. The clubhead works with this rotation of the body by moving slightly up and inside the target line.

### Pro Example: Erik Compton

In 1993, twelve-year-old Erik Compton came to my school. He was recovering from a tough heart transplant. Unable to play baseball, his father brought him over to try golf. He began working with one of my master instructors, Marie Salter. Using the building-block idea, Marie started Erik very slowly. Of course, that's really all he could manage. Week after week, Erik practiced a halfway-back-to-halfway-through swing. First, he learned Step 2 and how to make a one-piece takeaway. With juniors, we used imagery and visuals. I'm always huge on visuals. For Erik, the idea of handing a clubhead back into the catcher's glove worked great.

Marie had him feel and execute the movements of the upper body and the pelvis in coordination with the golf club. She taught him to keep the shaft between his arms going away to avoid rotation of the clubface. The turn of the shoulders and hips are what open the clubface. The wrists and forearms can roll the clubface open, which is a very bad mistake. Over time, Erik was making a very connected and super simple move to Step 2. Then he worked on impact, Step 6, by simulating a perfect position. Next, it was 7a and then 7b (extension position) just as described in this book.

Erik never lost this early training and within a few years he was swinging full out. By the time he was seventeen, he was the top-ranked junior golfer in America. He was the American Junior Golf Association's player of the year and a first-team All-American. He was the top recruit in America with scholarship offers to any top university of his choice. Erik chose the University of Georgia, where he played on a top-ranked team. He often roomed with Bubba Watson, which has provided some of my favorite golf stories.

Erik had a second heart transplant when he was twenty-seven, after having a heart attack in Miami. He called me as he was driving himself to the hospital knowing that he had suffered a heart attack. Erik wanted to tell me that he loved me and wanted to say goodbye in case he didn't survive. He made it to the hospital but collapsed before he could reach to the door. The hospital staff got him inside and saved his life, but his heart was weak, and we learned he was going to die without a transplant. For weeks, he stayed at Jackson Memorial Hospital and it looked bleak.

Many physical matchups must happen to get the right donor. Miraculously a heart became available, and Erik's surgery was successful. After the operation, Erik had a long recovery and the doctor told him golf was definitely over. One day he stopped over to see me and said he had shot a 66 at a nearby Miami course. I was amazed when he said he thought he might be able play on the PGA TOUR. Sure enough, a miracle happened. He won on the Web.com Tour, which qualified him for the PGA TOUR.

Then in 2013, Erik Compton finished runner-up (tied with Rickie Fowler) to Martin Kaymer in the U.S. Open at Pinehurst. I flew up for that fourth round to watch him play. If you knew Erik's journey, if you knew the medications he takes every day, if you knew what he does for the heart-transplant community, then you would know that Erik is a golf hero.

Erik Compton learned his golf swing segment by segment, piece by piece, step by step. His golf swing is a thing of beauty. It's simple and extremely powerful, and he does it without much practice.

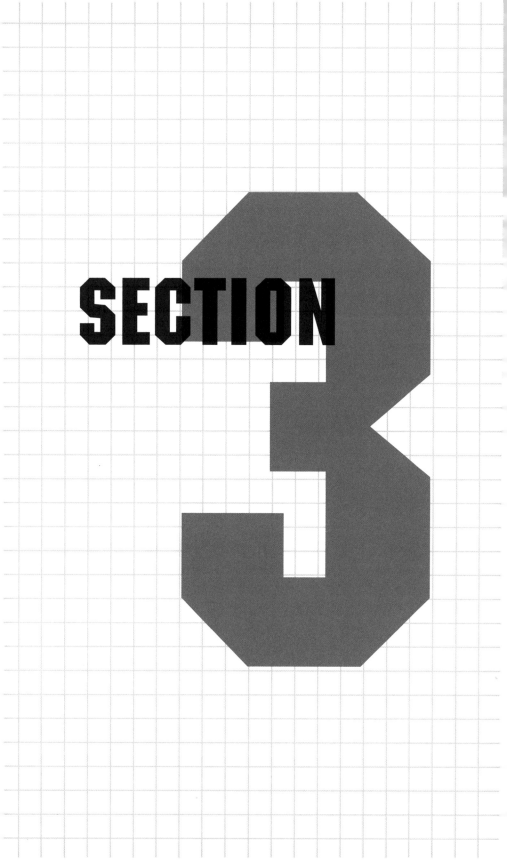

SECTION

3

## STEP 3

# LEAD ARM AND THE CLUBSHAFT FORM THE LETTER L

In our Jim McLean Golf School studies of tour pros, we noted with an iron shot that there is a distinct L shape created by a vast majority of golfers. Knowing that, I feel very comfortable that this is the best way to teach all golfers how to get into what we call Step 3.

There are variances of when golfers set their wrists—especially when they're swinging fairway metal woods and the driver. Jack Nicklaus and Greg Norman did not set the angle until later in the swing. In other words, no perfect L shape was formed at Step 3.

The takeaway set angle is variable, but we teach our golf-school students to set a vertical pitch—a steep angle at this position. This gives the feeling of a light club and stops the golfer from rolling the club, which is a common death move. A more vertical pitch in the backswing gives students the chance to shallow the shaft in the downswing, which is usually something they have never experienced.

By Step 3, the golfer's swing is fully loaded and ready to change direction moving toward the ball. At our golf schools, we have students hit shots from this loaded, three-quarter backswing position. We will practice Step 3 until the student is proficient, and then have them continue the swing smoothly all the way to Step 8 (the finish position).

**BUILD YOUR SWING**

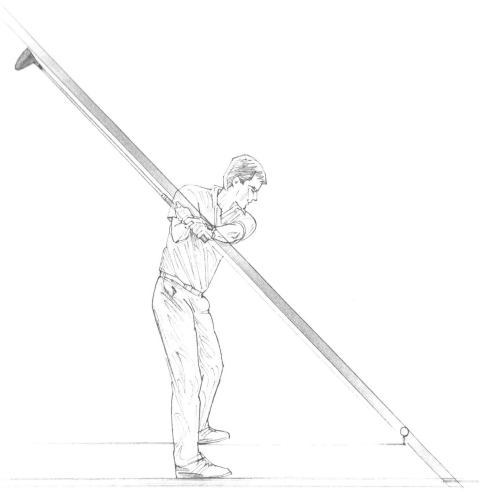

The shaft is on a 45 degree angle. Same knuckle count as at setup. It's a great way to feel the slot and understand swing plane.

## DRILL

Hit shots off a tee from the Step 3 position but at a slow rate of speed. For many amateurs, this is an easy drill. Make sure to go to a full finish in balance. Don't get discouraged, make sure to get that golf club in a good position at Step 3 before you start down.

## STEP 3 CHECKPOINTS

1. **Weight transfer is completed.** This means that by the time your lead arm reaches parallel to the ground in the backswing, the weight shift is complete.

2. **Pressure moves toward the heel.** As the golf club moves away from the target and is set at Step 3, pressure in the trail foot must not move into the toes. This mistake often occurs when the golfer's head moves toward the target line.

   When two-time PGA TOUR winner Lenny Mattiace had a bad skiing accident and tore ligaments in both knees, he lost strength in his quadriceps. I learned how important those muscles are, because Len could no longer stop pressure from moving into the toes of his trail foot. The lesson to take from Len's situation is to keep your legs strong and pay attention to the quads. They supply so much support to your ankles and feet during the swing. It took years for Len to recover.

3. **Keep the lead arm extended, but not tense.** It's possible to overextend the lead arm. It can disconnect from your chest. That's why I say to keep the lead arm nearly straight, but not tense. Sometimes when students hold the Step 3 position, the lead arm begins to shake. The reason for this is usually tension, but it could also be a weak arm.

4. **Count your knuckles.** I have students check their knuckle count on the top hand at address and at Step 3. If you see two knuckles on your top hand at address, you should see two knuckles at Step 3. If you don't, then you have either opened the clubface (you'll see three or four knuckles), or you have closed the club-

face (you won't see any). I came up with the concept of counting knuckles by teaching way too many amateurs who opened the clubface.

## JM Lesson: How Does the Clubface Open Excessively?

You can avoid the mistake of opening the clubface, a real swing killer, by first understanding how it happens. It's your lead wrist (the wrist on top of the grip) that causes this problem. When your lead wrist cocks vertically upward, the clubface will open. I teach my students to fix this problem by cocking the trail wrist (the one on the lower part of the grip) horizontally.

The late Claude Harmon taught many amateurs to flatten the lead wrist early in the backswing. The best way to do this is to cock the trail wrist horizontally, so by Step 3, the golfer would see less knuckles. This results in a strong or closed clubface. Mr. Harmon played with a bowed left wrist. He was a Masters champion.

I agreed completely with Mr. Harmon about how the wrists should cock. When we met and studied his idea, I had already seen too many amateurs with weak swings (caused by opening the face on the way back). His teaching reinforced my ideas of a square or slightly closed clubface being preferable to an open face (toe down). I first wrote about this in my book *The Eight-Step Swing*. It's a miracle move for many amateurs.

## STEP 3 DRILL

Get the shaft set at 45 degrees.

At Step 3, I draw a mental picture for my students using three lines. One is a vertical line, the wall of a building. The second is the ground (a horizontal line). The third is an angled line between the two, at 45 degrees. We put the shaft on the 45-degree angle with the clubface square. It's a very simple idea most students quickly understand. Keep in mind that this is only a drill to help put the shaft in a great position during the downswing.

### Explanation of "The 45" Slot Drill

Each of your golf clubs has a different lie angle. Only your driver is set at 45 degrees.

Your irons are more upright, with your lob wedge being the most upright, because it's the shortest.

However, that 45-degree angle happens to be a great way to explain and feel the "slot."

The slot is a position in the downswing that allows the golfer to be on plane and in position to deliver the golf club powerfully from inside the target line. By swinging the club at or near this 45-degree angle, you'll have a feel for slotting the club.

## CLUB SHAFT BALANCE

Another concept to consider at Step 3 is balancing the club. Many years ago, I worked with Joe Nichols, a top teaching professional in Phoenix. Joe was working with a number of PGA professionals and taught dawn to dusk. Joe also was a genius in helping the average golfer. He would place them near a fence and have them make a backswing trying to miss the fence. Of course, the amateurs would all swing into the fence at first. Joe would then explain the idea of balancing the clubhead above the shaft. The club feels light when it's vertical with the weight directly above the fulcrum. I've used this idea from Joe so many times to get my students to improve and develop more clubhead speed—no longer taking the club away flat and out of balance. A teacher might also work on getting your hand and club more in front of your chest, but the way you set the club at Step 3 is critical to adding power to your backswing motion. Almost all tour players take the club more vertical on the backswing and then shallow the shaft somewhat on the downswing.

The letter "L" at Step 3.

I do a lot of training with my students. Here's a "thumbs up" Step 3 drill.

**LEAD ARM AND THE CLUBSHAFT FORM THE LETTER L**

## Pro Example: Lenny Mattiace

When I started working with Len Mattiace, he was playing on a mini-tour called the Hooters Tour. Len had been a fantastic junior golfer and had made the U.S. Walker Cup team at age nineteen. He was a super hard worker and got every ounce out of his game. However, playing professional golf was proving very tough for Len. He came to me on a recommendation from another student of mine—Brad Faxon. That's how me met.

In 1993, we started a professional relationship that has turned into a lifetime friendship. Lenny Mattiace is one of the best human beings you could ever meet. The first time I saw him swing a golf club, I noticed several important flaws and we went to work. One of the first things I showed him was my drill that starts with the L-swing position at Step 3. It's a great drill for properly setting the club in the backswing. To complete the drill, I would have Lenny set the club perfectly at Step 3, and then whistle the club through the impact zone but stop at Step 7c. When he did this drill, his shots would rip it straight at his targets. You could hear the ball zing off the turf. Obviously, the shots did not go as far as they would with a full swing, but this training exercise had a great effect on his full swing.

When he went to the final stage of PGA TOUR Qualifying School, he did the drill every day after each round and then left. He hit no other golf shots, trusting that this training exercise was all he needed to have the feel to hit great shots when he played. He qualified for the PGA TOUR easily and went on to win two PGA TOUR events. The L-swing drill gets my students hitting the dead center of the clubface and improves Steps 7a, 7b, and 7c (post impact, extension, and exit positions).

## STEP 3 VS. STEP 5A (SHAFT POSITIONS)

The comparison between these two positions has interested me since I first started teaching. In fact, I wrote and compared these backswing and downswing positions in the first X-Factor book and described them in my series of TV shows on the Golf Channel. I wrote about how the shaft shallowed with almost every tour player. I showed how most PGA TOUR players flattened the shaft by Step 5, making it easier to hit good shots. With that said, here are a few top players that actually steepen the shaft on the downswing: Phil Mickelson, Rickie Fowler, and Raymond Floyd. You can be a great golfer and not shallow or flatten the plane.

Just remember that over 95 percent of tour pros flatten or shallow in transition.

## STEEPNESS AND SHALLOWING

The key to analyzing a swing plane is to check Steps 5b through 7b and determine a neutral swing direction (the measurement from 5b to 7b on the TrackMan launch monitor is basically halfway down to halfway through). The top ball-striker will have sufficient speed and consistently hit the center of the clubface. These are key elements of the swing analysis done at my golf schools.

The vast majority of great ball-strikers lay the club down into the slot in transition. Here's what happens and how to do it: When taking the club back, the pitch of the shaft is more vertical. A line through the shaft should point between the target line and the toe line. The left arm is in a corridor from 10 to 45 degrees inside the target line. I've described the shape of the backswing looking as though the hands work in a slight dish shape going up. Starting the downswing, the hands then move straight down plane to the backswing corner (at Step 5b delivery position).

Getting the clubshaft up and on plane. For your driver it's at 45 degrees.

In the downswing transition (described in Step 5a), the body has lowered. The initial move down is highly instrumental in a great swing. At this moment, the clubhead falls away from the target line and more behind the golfer. It's a move that is so natural to many gifted young golfers but hard to teach to the older golfer—especially those with a steep change of direction in their swings. It takes a very skilled teacher to get an older golfer to shallow the club correctly. It's so easy to do incorrectly, which frustrates the student. The key I often use for the older golfer is starting the club down with focus on the arms while slowing down the shoulders. Then they can flatten or shallow out the downswing plane.

Remember, we don't want to be too steep or too shallow.

## STEEP FROM THE INSIDE

This happens when golfers try to hit from the inside by dropping the hands and arms down behind the body. It's a somewhat common mistake, but it's definitely a death move. When the arms drop behind the body, the clubshaft must be steep to hit the ball. To change this, I teach the student how the trail elbow works in throwing a ball. The elbow swings slightly outward, just as it should in a golf swing.

## THE TWO CORNERS OF THE GOLF SWING

Not many golfers picked up on this two-corners teaching concept in *The Eight-Step Swing*. Think of a delivery position (Step 5b) as the back corner and the extension position (Step 7b) as the front corner. Examine these two corners and note if the shaft lines up parallel to your target line. There is a beautiful symmetry to each corner with the exception that the hands are higher at Step 7b. I did an entire DVD called *The Powerline*, which is a detailed description of the most important part of the golf swing. Notice that the hands are higher at Step 7b.

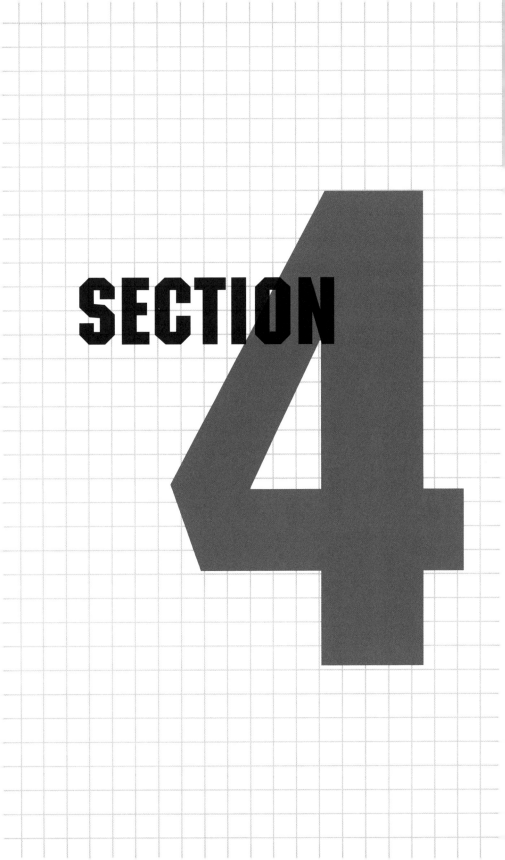

SECTION

4

# STEP 4
# TOP OF THE BACKSWING

In this book, the top of the backswing is defined as the moment when the clubhead stops its backward movement. That's the completion of the backswing. However, as I wrote in *The X-Factor*, I can argue that there is no top to the backswing. That's because the lower body has already begun the forward swing action as the club is still going back.

The great Sam Snead in the classic perfect top of the backswing (Step 4) position.

The top line of the McLean Cone represents Hogan's pane of glass.

I'm teaching a power X-factor coil.

**BUILD YOUR SWING**

DUSTIN "BOWED" WRIST
AT THE TOP

Dustin Johnson is in his unique super "bowed" position. I told a young Dustin to never let anyone change this. It's very powerful but requires matchups at impact.

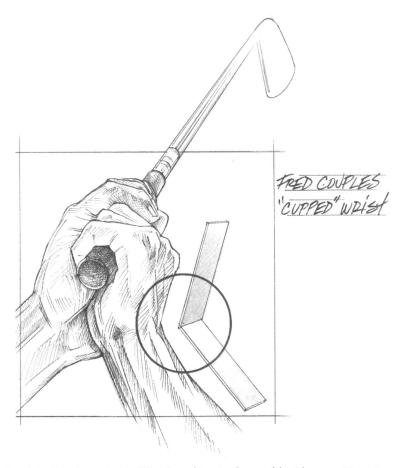

*Freddie Couples attained No. 1 ranking in the world with a position at the top that many would change. The cupped wrist open clubface and across the line. By looping and shallowing the shaft angle starting down (many do this), Freddie has played great golf his entire life. Many of my students rate his swing as their favorite.*

In my thirty years of playing and practicing with Ken Venturi, he often described this as a "two-way motion." Ken shared the concept with me, but it took years and many demonstrations to fully comprehend the ideas and concepts that he used to educate me on Ben Hogan's golf swing. Ken modeled his swing on Hogan.

The great Canadian golfer George Knudson used to sit on Venturi's golf bag and watch Ken hit balls for hours on end. George copied many of Kenny's golf movements, which Venturi had copied from Hogan. The influence of Hogan has been massive on all teachers.

I don't believe anyone understood the top of the backswing and transition better than Ben Hogan. At that time, no one had ever delivered information that deep into the mechanics and technique of a good golf swing. If you take away anything from Hogan, read what he said about the change of direction from backswing to downswing. The top modern golf-biomechanics experts have a great understanding of the correct sequencing and how the vertical ground force works.

My friend Jackie Burke also played many rounds with Hogan and studied him closely. Jackie Burke's partner in building Champions Golf Club in Houston was Jimmy Demaret, a three-time Masters champion. Jimmy was the closest friend Ben Hogan ever had. All three of these men were from Fort Worth, Texas. I was so fortunate to know these gentlemen and talk about Hogan with them. There's nothing like being out there on the range or golf course with the best in the game.

## BACKSWING TIME

The backswing takes time; it's not a fast movement. With practice, you can groove a backswing. This is something any golfer can improve. I love what Hogan wrote about it. He visualized a simple path that he could repeat. Hogan used the idea of a large pane of glass oriented on an inclined plane. The pane of glass rose up from the target line and rested on his shoulders. The pane had a hole in it, so Hogan's head was above it, but the rest of his body was under it as he stood in address posture.

Hogan grooved a backswing (just as you can) that stayed on the inclined plane. At the top of the backswing, Hogan wanted his lead arm to rest against the pane of glass. That is a great visual that many top players and teachers have used. Hogan thought this was the perfect position but said it was still acceptable if the left arm was slightly under the glass. What he didn't want was to break the glass when he swung. Hogan wanted depth with his arms to put them in a powerful position.

## ROLE OF THE TRAIL ARM

The trail arm controls the depth and height of your backswing and how to maintain a straight lead arm. To experience this, set up with your lead arm absolutely limp. Grab the thumb of that hand with the trail hand. Now using just the trail hand, mimic a backswing. You'll find that you can take the lead arm to any location. Ken Venturi always told me the right arm and right side controlled the backswing.

The trail elbow should be behind the golfer. This is an illustration of the right elbow position of Jack Nicklaus.

## JM Top Teaching Idea

Since my earliest days on the lesson tee, I've taught that "when the shoulders stop turning, the arms stop swinging." That's an idea that many modern teachers have taken from my books.

Many golfers from every skill level struggle with this concept. They allow the arms to keep swinging when the shoulders have halted. I've called this "arm run-off." I wrote about this concept in *The Eight-Step Swing*. This part of the book received a great deal of attention, and it was a subject I discussed in detail during live Golf Channel appearances and educational seminars I did around the world.

In the modern game, especially demonstrated by many of the top young PGA TOUR professionals, I'm seeing a big shoulder turn combined with a short arm swing. I like this very much. It's definitely an idea Tiger Woods picked up and used during his epic run of golf from the late 1990s into the 2000s. It's a great way to sync your swing and feel a very simple coil taking the club back. Remember: full shoulder turn, short arm swing! Think of Brooks Koepka, Justin Rose, Viktor Hovland, and Justin Thomas of the current top ball-strikers.

## Pro Example: Bernhard Langer

I gave a series of lessons to Bernhard Langer when he was playing the PGA TOUR in 2000. He had been experiencing a bad spell of golf and came to see me at Doral. This was before Track-Man, but I used a GOLFTEC swing analyzer to measure key factors of the swing in the impact zone, including path and swing speed. I had already measured hundreds of tour players on this machine when Bernhard came in for a lesson.

Before doing anything else, we sat down and talked about exactly what was happening with his game and what he was working on. I wrote everything down. He had been focusing very hard on his backswing. I asked him to show me some practice swings, and we went out on the range so I could videotape his swing. I asked what he thought of the driver shots he just hit, and he said they weren't great. But Bernhard really wasn't sure, so I had him hit a few more with his driver while monitoring them with the GOLFTEC machine. I told him to look at his swing speed. It was reading 100 to 101 miles per hour. At that time, many PGA TOUR players didn't pay too much attention to the speed numbers. I bluntly told Bernhard Langer, "What you have been working on is not getting it done. . . . You can't play on the PGA TOUR at that slow of a swing speed."

I told him he had lost the great Langer coil, and I pulled pictures from my library to show him his former swing. Since that time, his backswing had become all arms with too much lift. He was trying to set the club earlier in the backswing, which was narrowing his arc. I told him to forget this, and instead we worked on creating a much stronger coil at the top of the swing (Step 4). Obviously, there were things we did to get that stronger position, but my goal was to see him coil fully. This meant allowing a small amount of lateral shift into his right side and bracing the right leg. I asked him to put pressure into the right thigh and hip. These ideas apply in Steps 1–4, but they are most evident at Step 4, which is where I knew Bernhard would gain a lot of speed.

The progression of understanding key checkpoints in the golf swing is the best way to successful instruction. Bernhard went from 101 miles per hour to 108 that day. I knew he could swing successfully at that speed, and he did. Remember, at this time, he was still using steel shafts and hitting older balls with a shorter, 43-inch driver.

Sometimes even the great players need a kick in the pants. At the beginning of that first lesson, I questioned Bernhard on what he was thinking and told him that he couldn't play on the PGA

114

TOUR with 100 miles per hour clubhead speed. He definitely didn't want to hear that, but he responded immediately. The lesson went great, and I worked several more times with him that year. I'm good friends with Bernhard's longtime teacher, Willie Hoffman, who lives in Germany. I've also maintained my friendship with Bernhard Langer to this day. He's absolutely one of the finest human beings—and a Hall of Famer all the way.

## STEP 4 DRILLS: THE STOP AND GO

### Pro Example: Peter Jacobsen

I figured out this drill by watching a club professional working through some backswing issues. He would swing to the top, stop, and then change his clubface position and adjust his arms. Then he would repeat. I wondered if I could stop at the top briefly and then restart the swing and hit a shot. Through practice, I found I could make basically any backswing stop and then swing down and still hit the ball well. Knowing this, I started teaching my students with backswing issues how to stop and adjust, then swing. It worked great for many of them. Viktor Hovland is currently using this same drill. But of the many golfers I taught the stop-and-go drill, I think Peter Jacobsen benefited the most.

Peter and I became friends almost as soon as he got on the PGA TOUR. Peter was the first player to give me national attention. He came to see me during the Westchester Classic in 1982. I was the head professional at Sunningdale Country Club near Westchester Country Club, where the tournament was played. Peter finished second that year, losing when Bob Gilder made an incredible double eagle on the final hole. As with many other tour players, I saw Peter periodically at tour events in different locations. In 1992, Peter decided to leave the tour and take a top

115

commentator job with ABC. I was in California that year for the Tournament of Champions at La Costa (now Omni La Costa) in Carlsbad, and ABC was doing the broadcast. Carlsbad happened to be where Carl Welty lived, so I never missed that event. Carl and I would videotape players' swings all day and then study the tapes until two or three in the morning.

Anyway, Peter was doing the telecast, not playing, but he came to visit me as soon as he arrived at La Costa. When we saw each other, he gave a full account of his disappointing past year playing golf. I told him to come down to Carl's school the next day to do some work. He did, and I watched Peter hit shots. I remember being so surprised at how badly he hit them. I'm talking about a guy who was once one of the top ball-strikers on the planet. I wondered what happened to his swing.

There were a number of things I saw with Peter's technique I wanted to correct. One of the drills I suggested to help him get his swing back was the stop-and-go to improve his position at the top. We worked each day after the telecast. On the day before he left, I recorded all of Peter's PGA TOUR stats for his career on tour and brought them to his room. The stats were so impressive until the previous year or so. I explicitly told Peter, as a friend and teacher, "You can't stop playing on the tour. You can't go out at age thirty-eight with all of your talent. You just can't." Peter was still going to play events between telecasts, but I told him to quit ABC and go back on tour full time. I just knew he had so much more in the tank. He took my words to heart and soon after quit ABC. Peter played some nice tournaments in 1992 to finish the year as we stayed in touch. I saw him at numerous events.

The following year, 1993, Peter had his swing back and already had won two times before he got to Doral, where I was teaching. We worked there every day, and he almost won Doral too. He was leading after three rounds and was paired with

Greg Norman for the final day on Doral's Blue Monster. Peter finished second with a massive, boisterous crowd following them all the way. I vividly remember Peter practicing out of my "Superstation" hitting bay. He would aim at a pin and stripe shots that did not move. "I'm dotting the i," he said. I had never heard that before and asked what he meant. He explained that the flagstick was the lowercase *i* without a dot, and the golf ball was coming down right on top to provide the dot. That was supreme confidence. That's the kind of confidence needed to win on tour. Peter made the U.S. Ryder Cup teams in 1993 and 1995.

I can guarantee that the stop-and-go drill had to do a lot with Peter Jacobsen's success. He used that drill for the rest of his career. I should also note that Tiger Woods said the stop-and-go drill was one of the best drills Butch Harmon used during Tiger's 1997–2002 run.

## How to Do the Stop-and-Go Drill

Start by taking practice backswings in front of a mirror or have someone record them in slow motion (a smartphone video camera works nicely). Or have a teacher guide you to a great top-of-backswing location. I check everything at the stop position including balance, length of swing, weight, pressure, tension, clubface, and clubshaft locations. Once you can swing to the correct spot hold it for a full second and then swing through to the finish.

Practice hitting off a tee at first. Then you can start hitting shots. An 8 iron is a good club to use when you first try this drill. It can take some time before you can pause and then successfully hit the driver like Peter Jacobsen was doing when he was dotting the i. I've taught this drill to juniors like Lucy Li, who qualified for the U.S. Amateur at age ten and the U.S. Open at eleven. She is the youngest ever to play in that prestigious event. (Another student of mine, Lexi Thompson, previously was the youngest at age twelve.)

## The Role of the Right Arm (Trail Arm)

Ken Venturi emphasized the right arm in the takeaway and at the top. He taught me that it was the right arm and hand that supported the left arm at the top. If you disagree, try swinging your golf club to the top with just your left arm. Two things usually happen: the arm does not stay straight and the swing is very short. In contrast, take the club back with the right arm and see how easy it is to place the club wherever you want and as far back as you want. Two of my best teaching tips in creating a better backswing and keeping width and length to your swing are:

1. Take the club away with your trail side.
2. Turn your trail shoulder behind your right ear.

## Pro Example: Keegan Bradley

When Keegan Bradley came to see me in 2009, I had no idea who he was. His roommate in Orlando, Jon Curran, asked me to give him a lesson. I had worked with Jon since he was sixteen. Jon had reached No. 1 in the national junior rankings and was a promising young professional, but Keegan was pretty much unknown. He had never played in any USGA event or won any amateur events of consequence and had just graduated from St. John's University in New York. He was not an All-American or even an honorable mention at St. John's, which was hardly a recognized golf school. When Keegan arrived for his lesson, he wanted to make changes. He told me that he definitely needed to make improvements. I watched him hit balls and I videotaped his swing.

I agreed with Keegan that he needed to make some major changes.

It was a three-hour lesson, so I had time to give him three major things to change. The first was to eliminate 50 percent of his upper-body sway off the ball. The second was to eliminate the reverse-pivot in his lower body. The third was to change his shoulder plane. It was way too flat. I usually don't give a student that many difficult things to change, but I figured there was no downside. He was not playing well on the mini-tours. He was struggling on the Hooters Tour (now the SwingThought Tour) at the time. I thought if he could make the changes, there was a lot of upside. I also knew he would need to work hard on the short game, but we'd save that for another session if he ever came back. He told me he dreamed of playing the PGA TOUR.

I showed Keegan where I wanted to see his body and club at the top of the backswing. We repeated the Step 4 position over and over. It was a huge change. I took pictures of his top-of-back-swing positions before and after our work and gave him photos from both the face-on and down-the-target-line angles to study. I told him these were very big changes and to stick with the drills and exercises we had worked on. These changes could take months to ingrain, I said. He agreed and told me he would do the work. He left that day in a Ford Focus with the mirrors duct taped to the side of his car. I thought I might not ever see him again.

Three weeks later, he called and said he had won a Hooters event and a $30,000 check. He was ecstatic. At that time, Keegan had no money and that check will probably remain the most significant he ever cashed.

We started working full time after that, and he made it to the Web.com Tour (now the Korn Ferry Tour) in 2010. The following  year, he found himself on the PGA TOUR, and he won the AT&T

Byron Nelson tournament in Texas. That win came with a $1.1 million check and an invitation to the Masters Tournament the following year.

During the Byron Nelson that year, I worked with Keegan at my golf center in nearby Fort Worth. We were all so excited about that win. I had dinner with Keegan and his caddie, Pepsi, at a Dallas steakhouse after his victory. The owner recognized Keegan and gave us a private room. All the waitresses came in to get a picture with Keegan. It was an incredible evening. That week in Dallas had changed everything for him. What a difference a few years could make!

Later that year, I flew up to Atlanta and Keegan would go on to win a major, the PGA Championship in Atlanta. And in the fall, he won the Shark Shootout (now the QBE Shootout). At year's end, I went with Keegan to Bermuda, where he won the Grand Slam of Golf against the other major champions that year. He beat Rory McIlroy by one shot and was named the PGA TOUR's Rookie of the Year. In the next few years, Keegan would achieve the No. 1 ranking on the PGA TOUR in total driving and No. 1 in the overall stat category. Since 2011, nobody has driven the ball more consistently or better than Keegan Bradley.

The position Keegan achieves at Step 4 is very close to Jack Nicklaus's top-of-swing. I helped Keegan get his clubface square and his shoulders turned on the correct plane. A tall golfer like Keegan cannot afford a flat shoulder turn. Keegan had to feel keeping the left shoulder down and feeling the right shoulder go up and behind the right ear. When we made this change to Keegan's swing, his lead arm automatically went higher with the thumbs directly underneath the shaft.

When the hands are in this position, the clubface appears slightly open. When the clubshaft is more vertical, the face looks open. Conversely, when the hands and clubshaft are flatter, the clubface will appear closed. It's very important for the teacher to understand clubface orientation at different stages of the swing and in different locations.

When the club is set correctly at Step 4, it sure makes it easier to transition the club down and strike the ball great. That being said, look at the many different positions great players are in at the top. They are amazingly different. So take into consideration your height, age, and flexibility. This will help tremendously in correcting your big miss.

My instructors and I understand that Step 4 is an important position, but there are variables based on grip, length of arms, torso, legs, size of the chest, flexibility of the golfer, and overall strength and size of the player. Injuries also play a role, so it's up to the teacher and player to adjust based on these factors.

## HERE ARE A FEW THINGS YOU SHOULD FOCUS ON

**The shoulders turn more than the hips.** In Keegan's swing, there is a huge differential. He turns his shoulders more than 100 degrees from their address position while restricting his hip turn to less than 50 degrees. We worked very hard on his hip rotation. I don't think most golfers understand that there is some lateral motion in the backswing. I had Keegan imagine that his spine reached the ground. I told him the bottom part of the spine must slide slightly away from the target. This was a visual that Keegan locked into. It stopped his reverse-pivot and helped him load correctly into his trail side. Remember, you don't turn or spin the hips to the top of your backswing—that causes a reverse-pivot and kills your long-iron and driving game. If you watch yourself swing in a mirror, you'll see that turning the hips can make your trail hip move toward the target. Practice turning into your trail side, so that the lead hip stays in the position it was in at address. It should not reverse-pivot nor slide or sway excessively from the target.

Before you reach the top of the swing, the lower body should already start moving in the other direction. Few players change direction earlier than Keegan Bradley. The golf club should feel like it's slowing or quiet for a moment at the top of the swing—like it's stalling. This was the great concept I learned from Ken Venturi. He used this description of the transition, and it can work for so many golfers. It definitely worked for Keegan. He always gave the impression that the club was moving very slowly at the top while the lower body initiated the downswing. In Keegan's swing, you see no extra movement of the club after his body completes the backswing. When the arms take over at Step 4 and lift the club, or the club loosens in the hands, there is a disconnection between the arms and body—causing a huge power leak.

See how Lexi Thompson's right hand supports the club? The right arm determines width, not the left.

Rory McIlroy at Step 4 with an iron.

**Ratios.** From my studies on the X-Factor, and the biomechanics that follow, we see that all top ball-strikers generate a significant differential between shoulder turn and hip turn. In biomechanics, they describe it as rib-cage turn compared to shoulder turn. That might be a better way to phrase it. Regardless, you always see the shoulders turn significantly more than the hips. There are safety zones with the X-Factor, because some very long hitters do not have a huge shoulder turn by Step 4. These players have a very braced lower body. The shoulders might turn only 85 degrees, short of the old model of 90 degrees for a standard pro turn. Yet, the shoulder/hip differential is significant. What most do not see is that these long hitters start the hips early in the downswing and increase their X-Factor by 15 to 20 degrees. I called this "stretching the X." The fact is, all good ball-strikers stretch the X. Some do it only a few degrees, while

**TOP OF THE BACKSWING**

others we measured stretch up to 28 degrees. Dr. Rob Neal, a top biomechanics expert, came to work for me from 2003–14 and his team constantly measured golfers' movements at Doral. What we found was that the numbers established in the original X-Factor writings were very close. There was no doubt that establishing a strong X-Factor at Step 4 was critical to power golf.

Trail-knee action. I always stress to my students the idea of bracing the trail side, focusing on the role of the trail knee to maintain some flex. With Keegan, we worked on a flexed trail knee similar to what Jack Nicklaus and Tiger Woods employed. There are certainly differences in how much top golfers flex the knee, but it's because the knee moves differently from player to player. You should never try to keep that knee frozen. It should be flexed and move when you coil properly. There are good players who straighten the trail knee, but I hate to see golfers lock that leg. If a golfer makes a big hip turn, the trail knee is going to straighten. I spent three days with Sam Snead at his home in West Virginia doing a video series, and we talked extensively about leg action. I noticed that Sam straightened his right knee in the backswing, and I asked him specifically about it. He said it might look straight, but he never locked it. I've heard some teachers say that Sam locked the knee, but that's not true.

Jordan Spieth and Matthew Wolff are other players who straighten the trail knee, but I don't think they lock it. So even the players who straighten the trail leg they do not lock that knee. If they did, it would cause the trail hip to rise too high and put too much tension into the hips. The takeaway here is to maintain at least a little flexibility in the trail knee.

Watch Rory McIlroy, Tiger Woods, Dustin Johnson, and Justin Thomas on TV. They all have braced the trail knee while maintaining flex. It's part of how they generate power using X-Factor coil. I often advise students to lift the heel of the lead foot going back to improve coil. Actually, many top ball-strikers do this, too. The key is to do what is necessary to make a full coil and create a significant differential between the hips and shoulders. If lifting the lead heel helps, that's okay.

Hogan's famous pane of glass. The most interesting golf illustration of all time. Tiger's left arm is up against the glass, and so is the clubface (Step 4).

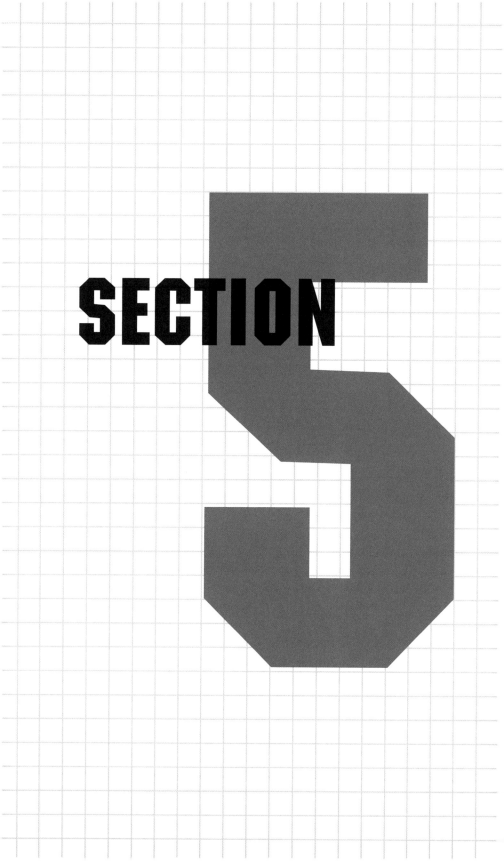

SECTION

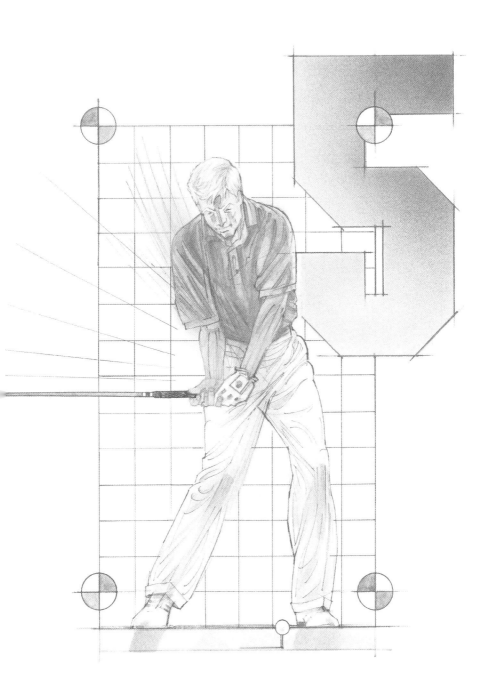

# TRANSITION

Transition is perhaps the key move in golf and our pro example does it effortlessly.

## THE WORLD-CLASS MOVE

When I was at the University of Houston, Ben Hogan would come down to practice at nearby Champions Golf Club with Jackie Burke. That's when I was able to watch the great man in person. His change of direction is considered by most top teachers as one of the best ever. At the same time, Lee Trevino was bursting onto the scene. I remember actually hearing Ben Hogan compliment Trevino before he won his first U.S. Open. Trevino went from a closed clubface at the top to a shallow-and-perfect delivery position by rotating his left forearm and dropping his right shoulder at Step 5a. Hogan and Trevino had opposite wrist positions and extremely different clubface positions at the top, yet both delivered the club perfectly time after time. They did it with a great transition, and that is why I study and teach this move with a very watchful eye. I spent a lot of time working on transition with Lexi Thompson and Keegan Bradley. Lexi comes from a deep Step 4 position, while Keegan comes from a much more vertical position. Both are the best drivers on their respective tours. Both make a world-class move starting down.

I first heard the term "world-class move" from John Schlee. John was a terrific tour player and later opened a golf school in the 1970s. He admired Ben Hogan and based his golf swing on what he gleaned from Hogan. The main idea I took from Schlee was the term "world class move" describing how the club shal-

I've always used other sports to teach golf. Here is a fabulous image of the infielder in baseball changing direction. He has fielded the ball and planted the trail foot from the outside of that foot first, and then to the inside of the foot. The lead foot has shifted pressure forward creating the huge gap between his legs. The hips are forward, but the shoulders coiled. The left shoulder is still down and his hand is on top of the baseball. In an instant, the left shoulder will rise, and the player will throw a sidearm rocket to first base. Remember that trail foot digs in and can actually rotate externally in the change of direction. If you are so inclined, you can try a half sidearm half underhanded throw to get the feel for golf.

lowed starting down. This means the clubhead falls behind the golfer or behind the hands, as the lower body sits down at the start of the downswing. To be clear, the clubhead falls behind the hand path starting down. That's a huge part of the magic move. To me, the world-class move is having the clubshaft fall "into the slot" where the swing is totally "on go." When you transition correctly, you're in perfect position to hammer the golf ball and hit it straight. I wrote *The Slot Swing* in 2009 describing in detail how players slot the club from different positions at the top of the backswing.

## COUNTER FALL

An extremely subtle move starts at Step 5a but is a continuous movement through Step 5b (delivery position) and Step 6 (impact). My friend and a great teacher, David Lee, termed it "the counter fall."

The counter fall is the move away from the target line in the downswing. Here's a synopsis: The average human arms weigh approximately twenty pounds. So think about how much force is being applied forward, toward the golf ball in the downswing with the arms and club. It's natural for the average golfer to be pulled forward when they try to hit hard, to lose balance. The reason for losing balance is starting out of sequence, with the arms or shoulders. You can add in "tension" in the arms and shoulders, which invariably results being off plane and all types of mishits. To avoid losing balance, the amateur will stop the body and swing easier.

Top ball-strikers counter fall, meaning they have an opposing force moving away from the target line. This slight backward fall off vertical is extremely difficult to see. But it happens in all sports involving hitting or throwing. It's easy to see in the soccer-style kicker in football. You can see it in a baseball throw, but in golf, it's indistinct. To do this in the golf swing, have the sensation of weight moving to the left heel or turning the left hip and the left side away from the target line. The top ball-striker falls forward starting down and then away from the target line, or off vertical. This opposing force keeps the top golfer in balance where they can comfortably hammer the golf ball. Poorer players are off balance, and to avoid moving too far to the toes, slow down their swings.

Ben Hogan lowers and counter falls away from the target line. The arms drop and the club falls into the slot.

**BUILD YOUR SWING**

At Step 5a (the delivery position halfway down) there should not be further lateral motion. An idea I use to stop a student over sliding is to feel pressure in the right heel as they start down, and work on the left hip rotating strongly away from the target line.

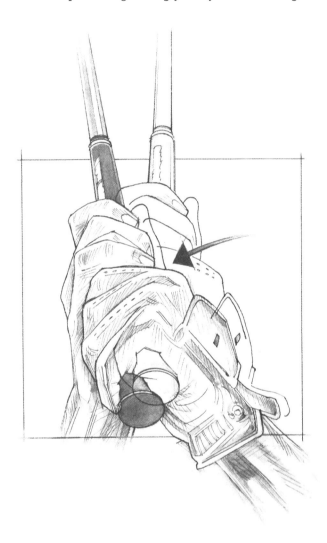

At the top of the backswing. This is a great pro trick move. Mickey Wright (considered to have perhaps the best golf swing of all time) wrote about this move. Squeeze the last two fingers of the top hand to have the clubhead fall behind the hands.

**TRANSITION**

In baseball, the bat shallows or flattens to nearly horizontal. In golf the shallowing is less, but it is critical.

**BUILD YOUR SWING**

## HAND PATH

I'll check all my students by simply watching their hand path both up and down as they swing. Starting down, I might see some major mistakes. The hands should be the last thing to move in your forward swing to have the correct kinematic sequence. The correct order is feet to start the transition motion, then the knees, hips, shoulders, and finally the arms and hands.

That's the correct sequence. If the hands follow, then the hand path should not drop flatter. The only time this is acceptable is if the arms are out and away in the backswing, like Trevino or McIlroy. In all other cases, your hands and arms will get stuck behind the body, a common mistake. Dropping the hands inside starting down will cause your path to be too far from inside the target line. Trevino changed everything by aiming his body fifty yards left at setup. Since the hands are quiet at the top, the hand path in a great golf swing should either be straight back down or usually slightly outside the path taken in the backswing.

### Hand Path Review

The hands go up in a slight dish-shape motion as the left arm elevates. But on the downswing, the hands take a straight path toward the ball. It can be called a straight-line to impact. Remember that the golf club does the opposite. The shaft flattens on the downswing.

### Shaft Tip-Over

When the shaft moves over the plane and into a vertical angle starting down, you're dead in the water. I call this "shaft tip-over" and it's my top-of-the-list death move in the golf swing. This mistake happens because the trail arm might be locked, and the golfer is unable to move the elbow forward. The other culprit is starting the trail shoulder too high and outward toward the target line.

## THE LEFT-SIDE DRILL

This is a drill I've used to put the golfer in a powerful position. It's specific to the scissor effect at impact, but I've found it highly useful to set up synchronizing this action by teaching left-side control.

**Left-arm-only drill.** This will get you into a backswing position that will help you move powerfully into and through impact. It will give you the opportunity to effectively use the scissors motion.

First, take the club back to the L position with only the lead arm, but make sure you coil your torso with the arm swing. Don't take the club back with just your forward arm!

The L position is defined by the arm swinging to halfway back, or parallel to the ground. Note that the left arm will be slightly inside the target line at this step. The wrist sets the club at a 90-degree angle to the arm. It's a full wrist set. You will quickly find that keeping the arm straight is extremely difficult if you don't coil with the swing. Keep the arm close to the torso, relatively straight, and set the wrist.

When you set the wrist, make sure to set it properly. You must not vertically cock the left wrist. That puts the clubface wide open. The left wrist is very close to flat, or even slightly bowed. The right wrist must set horizontally. The effect of this (for some) correct wrist set is a square clubface. The club shaft will point skyward, neither straight up nor straight flat to the ground. I'd much rather it be more toward vertical.

The flat shaft angle is a death move! Make no mistake, the wide-open clubface at this position is also a golf death move!

Halfway between vertical and horizontal is 45 degrees. That's basically the slot you want in the downswing, so this drill is tremendous for finding the slot.

Most tour players are slightly vertical on the backswing and then allow the club to fall into the slot on the downswing. You will find this movement critical to making good contact. This is a power move of the shaft in a great golf swing. Doing this drill correctly will do wonders for discovering coil, left-arm extension, and clubface control. When you do it well, you can move to the second part of the left-arm-only drill.

Next comes one of the key moves in golf. Since you've done the first part of the drill correctly, now initiate the forward move with a lateral shift of the hips. Do not immediately turn the hips. Instead put pressure into your front foot at the ball of that foot. This will quickly show you an important part of the swing. The arm responds poorly if the body is tense—then the golfer will use the arms and hands independently and throw the club off plane, either over the plane or under the plane, but always variable.

Finally, unwind the lead hip and notice how the arm falls slightly outward toward the ball. Be sure to keep that lead arm into the chest and not away from the body. The left hip moves weight away from target line, while the shaft falls onto the power plane. This is a counterbalancing effect. This effectively allows the golfer to stay in balance and not have everything fall forward, toward the toes. The shaft that has fallen slightly behind the hand path will now start to square up to that path and square up the clubface. In time, you will be able to hit some beautiful short shots just using the left arm.

## No Stop at the Top

Great ball-strikers are always in motion, meaning they do not stop at the top. It might appear that there's a slight pause at the top, and I'm often teaching a quiet position at the top, but the truth is something is always moving. Like Venturi said, it's the two-way move. While the club is reaching the end of its backward motion, the lower body has started to reverse direction. The stop-and-go drill I often teach to better players is in an effort to have them gather (or stall) at the top. I want them to feel soft or passive arms in the change of direction. Top ball-strikers start from the ground up by employing this move.

## THE FIRST X

I purchased one of the first video-recording machines (a Sony Betamax) in New York in 1979 and started a lifetime study of golf swings. One of my first discoveries was drawing a line on the backswing shaft plane and comparing the downswing plane at the same location. All the tour players shallowed the shaft plane, meaning the downswing plane was flatter or more laid off than backswing shaft plane.

In addition, I observed that the hand path almost always moved slightly outward in transition. In other words, the shaft plane and the hand plane usually work in the opposite way. By tracing the backswing hand path, I saw a slight but obvious dish shape—or described another way, a curved path to the top of backswing (from Step 2 to Step 4). Starting the downswing, the hand path takes a straight line path to the delivery position in Step 5a. This is the first corner of the swing. I detailed this in my earlier books and at teaching summits, but only recently has it come into prominence.

Several years ago, Dr. Sasho McKenzie did a biomechanics study on the easiest and most efficient way to square the club-face at impact. In a basic explanation, the center of gravity of the clubhead relative to the hand path drops behind the hand path. In this way, the center of mass wants to line up with the hand path making it easier to square the clubface at impact. Of course, this is exactly what I saw in the world's top ball-strikers. The lines crossed forming the letter X.

## DEATH MOVE

One of the main JM death moves is shaft tip over. That's when the amateur golfer does the opposite of the above. Meaning the shaft steepens on the downswing in a vertical orientation. Note: you can be steep from an inside hand path as well as the more common outside hand path. Both are killers!

How the body creates power in golf is extremely complex. To simplify it, I've had success teaching students using the main sources of power:

1. Weight shift
2. Rotation
3. Arm swing
4. Wrist action

### Explanation of Kinematic Sequence

The feet start the transition into the downswing, then the pelvis, then the shoulders, then the arms, and finally the wrists and hands. I put the feet first in my description, not the pelvis. This is because the feet use the ground and push into the ground. This is a key component to the movement.

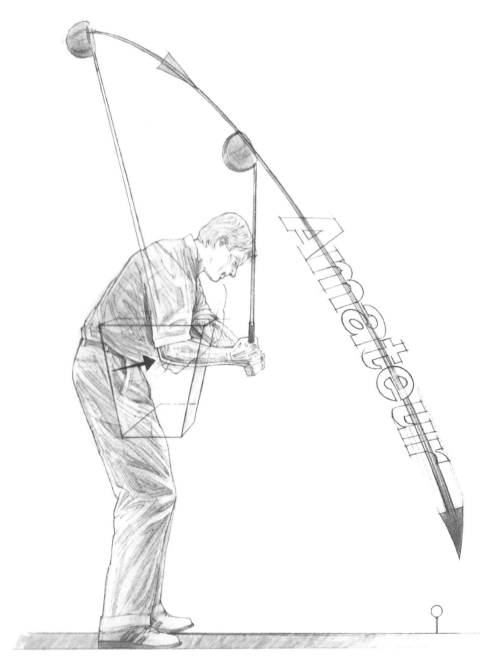

Shaft tip-over is a major death move. Usually with the club face open.

**BUILD YOUR SWING**

It's a chain action, as Ben Hogan wrote so well in the 1957 classic *Five Lessons*. If you look at the medical descriptions of body planes and an explanation of rotational forces, it becomes complicated beyond what is necessary to hit a golf ball at the highest level. Simplicity is the truest form of genius, something people like Einstein and Steve Jobs explained. We want a young child to understand the golf swing.

The shaft points over the target line at Step 5a. Most think it points directly at the target line but it does *not* in a top-class swing.

## TWO SEPARATIONS IN TRANSITION

There are two key separations that occur in transition. The first is the hips or pelvis moving toward the target before the shoulders. The second is the hands from the shoulders.

We see this at Step 5b, where the hands are farther away than at 5a. At the beginning of transition, do not throw the hands away from the trail shoulder, nor move them closer. At this early stage of the forward swing, keep the hands passive, maintaining the distance you had at the top.

## HIP/WALL DRILL

Take your golf posture, placing both hip pockets against a wall. Now make your backswing turn keeping the right hip pocket against the wall. You should feel pressure. Now start the transition forward. Lower your body as you turn the left hip pocket to the wall. At this point, both hips are against the wall again. This will be a very different feeling for many golfers. It will take many repetitions, especially for any golfer who has inward extension, meaning the hips move toward the ball. In this drill, you would incorrectly feel your hip pockets moving off the wall.

## PRESSURE-PUMP DRILL

From the top of your backswing, start your transition forward focusing on your feet. I always suggest doing this drill from a good backswing position. Key your forward transition by shifting pressure to the center of both feet. When you make this move, you might feel your pelvis going toward the target. You will also have the urge to move your arms and the club. Resist this feeling and consciously hold the hands back. Feel as though your hands are hanging in the air. This gives you the correct feeling of sequencing the start down.

## Pro Example: Webb Simpson

Webb Simpson's father asked me to work with Webb when he was a junior golfer. We had walked together at a junior golf event watching our sons play. Webb was already a terrific player but was off his game. I agreed, and Webb came to see me.

In those days, I had a golf school at Weston Hills near Fort Lauderdale, Florida, and that's where I worked with Webb. He would come see me periodically and stay at our Weston home. Later, he would attend Wake Forest University with my oldest son, Matt.

The most important thing I ever worked on with Webb was his transition move. Back then, when Webb changed directions, he would hang back and drop the club too far inside and under the plane. This poor movement resulted in a big inside-out swing direction. As a young junior, the inside-out path works great to help hit the ball farther without needing a lot of physical strength. But as you grow older and develop speed through increased muscle mass, it's a very unreliable way to swing the club. A severe inside-out path leads to misses far to the right (for a right-hander), big hooks, and the dreaded two-way miss. This was happening to Webb.

Over numerous sessions in Florida and some at Wake Forest, Webb and I worked hard on his downswing. I keep all my notes on every student and in looking back, it's fun to see how Webb progressed in changing his swing plane to a neutral path.

I think our best training sessions came by working with his wedge. When we started, he took almost no divot and his wedge shots hooked a lot. You probably know that it's quite unusual to hit hooks with a wedge, because the loft of the club greatly reduces sidespin. It's the easiest club to hit straight.

I didn't have a TrackMan when I worked with Webb, but I knew his swing path was far too inside out by the way he was hitting hooks. By careful placement of a video camera, I could compare Webb to top tour players. That's the way I learned to teach from Carl Welty. We used perfect camera angles to film tour players at PGA events. Since we filmed exactly the same way, we could do accurate detailed research. Checking a plane was perhaps the most important thing we looked for on video, and it all started at transition (Step 5). Webb dropped his right shoulder back and under, which I saw as a fatal flaw using a pitching wedge. To correct this, I had Webb feel as though he was going over the top of the plane and hitting much more down on the golf ball. I asked him to hold off the clubface from rotating closed and to hit low fades. We did this at slow swing speeds. I had Webb start his transition by moving into his left leg and getting his weight off his trail leg.

This was a big change and is a remedy reserved mostly for better golfers who swing excessively inside out. That's rare to see in amateurs. The goal was to get Webb on the correct downswing plane to improve compression and to eliminate the push hook. I'm sure I got Webb closer to a much better golf swing with good ideas and drills to improve his path and impact alignments. It's been great to see his success on the PGA TOUR, including winning a U.S. Open.

144

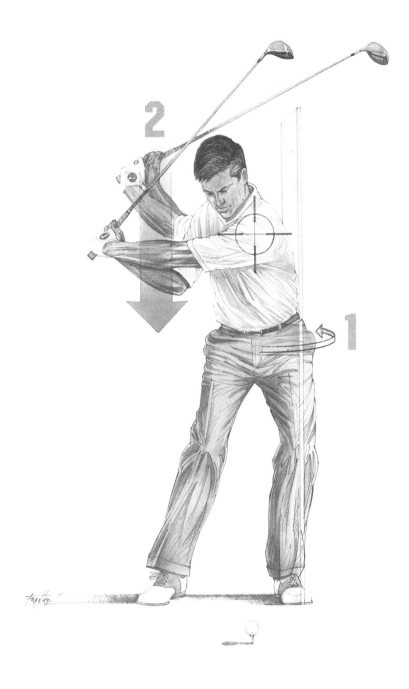

Simple idea of good sequence. The 1, 2 action happens simultaneously. It's not two separate moves.

**TRANSITION**

# THE POWER-DELIVERY POSITION

I've described this position as the corner of the downswing. It's the lowest point of hand path. Most amateurs never reach the corner, because the hands do not get low enough. I've taught this on-line delivery position for decades. It's important to understand the position of the left wrist. I want to see the wrist in a power position, meaning it's flat or slightly bowed. Ben Hogan called it supination of the lead wrist. When the left wrist is in the power position, the right wrist will be cocked, fully back, and loaded to create a powerful blow into the back of the ball.

## 5A TO 5B RIGHT LEG ACTION

As I explained and illustrated in *The X-Factor Swing*, weight should push down into the right leg as the transition from backswing to downswing begins. It only happens for a millisecond before the golfer fully shifts his or her weight into the lead leg.

This can be a very natural, athletic move that creates more leverage for the shot. Unfortunately, athletic moves might not be natural or easy for the average golfer. But to visualize it, think of how a baseball infielder catches a ball as he moves away from second base. That player will catch the ball, stop his momentum with the trail leg, turn, and then step into his left leg before firing the ball over to the first baseman. If you slowed down this acrobatic movement, you could see how his right leg pushes down into the ground as his left leg starts to move toward first. You would even see weight on the outside of trail foot in this throwing action. I see this in some of the power players in golf too. Hogan wrote about the throw from second base to first. The throw is half underhand and half sidearm. Just like the golf swing, the second baseman's throw requires a momentary separation of the hips (pelvis) from the shoulders. He's stretching the differential between the hips and shoulders—stretching the X by digging in with the outside portion of his trail foot.

## FOOTWORK

Two things I've noticed that nobody talks about:

1. **Weight shifting to the outside of the trail foot in the backswing or just as the player changes direction.** Going on top of the back foot is fine, but I noticed Bobby Jones, Sergio Garcia, and other top players going to the outside of the back foot at the completion of the backswing, or just when they start down. My longtime student George Zahringer (U.S. Walker Cup member) always did this and I never took it away. He did not practice very much and has been a great amateur for forty years on the national scale.

2. **The quiver (up and down) action of the trail foot near and through the impact zone.** Many great players have the back foot rise, come back down, and then rise again. I determined that it was the stall point from the hips stopping the forward move and reversing direction away from the target. The quiver in the trail foot is just a reaction to powerful hip action.

Without waiting to see impact, I can accurately predict what a student will look like when the ball is struck and the type of release action they will likely employ. How? I observe the clubshaft location, the height of the hands, and the orientation of the clubface.

The slot swing. What a great place! If the clubface is more closed (toe down), the golfer will have less face rotation through impact which is okay. (The drag release). When the shaft is parallel to the ground and parallel to the target line, you have the first side of the powerline. Clubface is square. On go!

This is why I say transition is the moment of truth. It largely predetermines how the golfer will strike the ball. The pictures show an inside delivery, an on-line delivery, and an outside (over-the-top) delivery.

*Here is an absolute fundamental. The downswing arc is inside the backswing arc.*

Remember, to properly analyze your golf swing on video, you must have your camera or phone placed directly down the target line and far enough behind you (at least eight yards) to ensure you can diagnose what's happening. Placing the camera too close will skew the appearance of the delivery alignments.

When we analyze video of the transition, we look at two club elements:

1. The club's shaft, which is ideally pointed down the line and parallel to the target line.
2. The orientation of the clubface (open, square, or closed).

I want to see the clubface square between 5a and 5b.

I also always check my student's body position and arm locations at 5b. The reason I look at them is because a student can deliver the club parallel to the target line but have their hands and arms too high. This is a common high-handicapper mistake.

*Powerful delivery position. Trail heel slightly off the ground. Trail knee kicking outward. Square clubface.*

**BUILD YOUR SWING**

## MISTAKES

I usually see collapsed arms (arms pulled inward close to the body) with this poor 5b position. These mistakes go hand in hand. If you compare the setup angles (Step 1a) to the position of the body at delivery (Step 5b), the golfer will be taller (straightening, otherwise known as lifting out of the shot). For this mistake, I prescribe these drills:

1. Focus on retaining the setup angles and "staying down" while swinging. All golfers should feel their feet applying pressure into the ground at Step 5b.
2. From the top of the swing, the student drops the right shoulder, right elbow, and right arm in tandem (no club is needed). The student should not lose the angle of the right wrist.

It's an amazing feel for most golfers. They've never understood, or more importantly, *felt* this move. I show them how the feet and the hip girdles provide a free ride starting down, combined with dropping the right elbow close to the right hip.

### Head Drop and Upper-body Compression

Announcers have criticized Tiger's head drop for decades, but most great ball-strikers drop their head in the downswing. It's a natural, athletic, power move. Remember, most TV announcers are not trained golf instructors. They are often caught off guard when a tour swing is slowed down, and what they think they see a mistake. Often it is not. I wrote an article on compressing the chest coming into impact in the 1990s. It seems to me that chest compresses. Also, the back and shoulders get rounded, not like setup. Nobody seems to ever comment on this.

The head drops, and the shoulders compress for a majority of great players.

## THE CRITICAL GEOMETRY FROM 5B TO 7B

It's extremely useful to see the delivery position (Step 5b) to the extension position (Step 7b) with impact coming between those points. Most amateurs I teach never get to an acceptable extension position (7b). They don't know what good extension feels like or what it should look like. One way of teaching extension is to put the student into the position. I start by explaining that this is the closest the clubhead will be to the target. Both arms are straight, but the left arm is not overextended because your right arm can't reach the overextended left arm.

The right wrist is angled down, and the club shaft is an extension of the right arm. Look closely at the body angles, paying

*Put yourself into a good extension position, and this will automatically improve your (5b) delivery position.*

**THE POWER-DELIVERY POSITION**

attention to the right foot. You roll off the inside of the right foot. The heel is in front of the toe. This is caused by the required lateral slide of your left hip. The left hip has bumped forward and rotated.

Depending upon age and flexibility, the amount of hip rotation can vary greatly from golfer to golfer. I evaluate this with each student. Less hip rotation means the student needs more wrist hinge and a more active arm swing to make up for the loss of power from less body rotation.

Regardless of how much the hips rotate, study the leg and knee action in the illustration on the previous page.

Good players will stay in their framework through Step 7b. Look at this illustration to see the right-side bend in the player's body. This is a biomechanics term for the forward angle of the body toward the target line. This forward angle closely mirrors the set-up angle. Now look at the shoulder angles. A young, flexible golfer will have a large angle with the left shoulder elevated much higher than the right. Again, I use my 45-degree angle as a guide.

The arms will be extending forward while your chest and spine are pulling backward.

## THE POWERFUL REVERSE SLOT

### Pro Example: Bruce Lietzke

I lived with a future great PGA TOUR player, Bruce Lietzke, when we were in college at the University of Houston. After that, we roomed together on the mini-tours. Bruce went on to win fourteen PGA TOUR events, plus the U.S. Senior Open. He was No. 1 in the total-driving statistic on tour nine times and was always near the top in greens in regulation. He was fully exempt on the PGA TOUR for twenty-eight straight years. Bruce was always a gifted ball-striker. He got the nickname "Leaky" in college because he hit a fade on every shot. It wasn't a weak slice, rather a power fade. I'll be referring to the power fade with the release of the club in Steps 7a, 7b, and 7c.

With Bruce Lietzke's swing, you could see the fade path at this step very clearly (if the camera is placed correctly). If there is any one important piece of advice I have passed down to all of my teachers, it's the details involved in camera placement. If the clubshaft is directly parallel to the target line, you would be in the perfect powerline position. Bruce had his clubhead just a

The classic reverse slot used by the great Bruce Lietzke, who led the PGA TOUR in ball-striking statistics numerous times. Others using this type of slot swing included Bobby Jones, Sam Snead, Craig Stadler, Marc Leishman, Viktor Hovland, Hale Irwin, and many more.

*When the club gets too far outside the hands at delivery position (5b), you will pull or slice shots.*

fraction out which gave him that reliable fade. He could repeat that path time after time. I have taught that Lietzke action to many of my long-hitting advanced golfers as a more dependable shot pattern.

### The Fade Position

In looking at an on-line delivery from down the target line, the clubhead blocks out the hands and the shaft is parallel to the line. In Lietzke's delivery, the clubhead is just slightly outside the hands. This is absolutely key to hitting a fade. I intuitively knew this, but when you see the position, it really makes sense.

When I worked with recent U.S. Open champion Gary Woodland in 2015 and 2016, he said he wanted to hit a fade and move away from the draw he had been relying on the past few years. I showed him video of Lietzke, and then we went to work practicing this position. I told Gary how Tom Kite and I worked on this position for six months in 1992, the year he won the U.S. Open.

Tom did it by feeling the right arm push out, meaning he straightened the right arm earlier in the downswing. That was a good feel for Gary as well, but he and Kite already had a huge amount of lag in their swings. Other players have said they like to feel the trail shoulder move toward the target line sooner. The last thing you want to do to fix a delivery that comes from too far inside is drop the right shoulder.

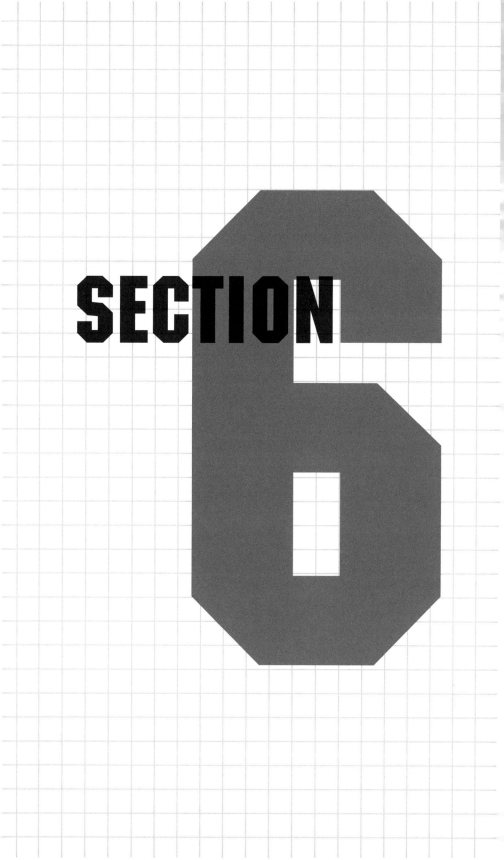

SECTION 6

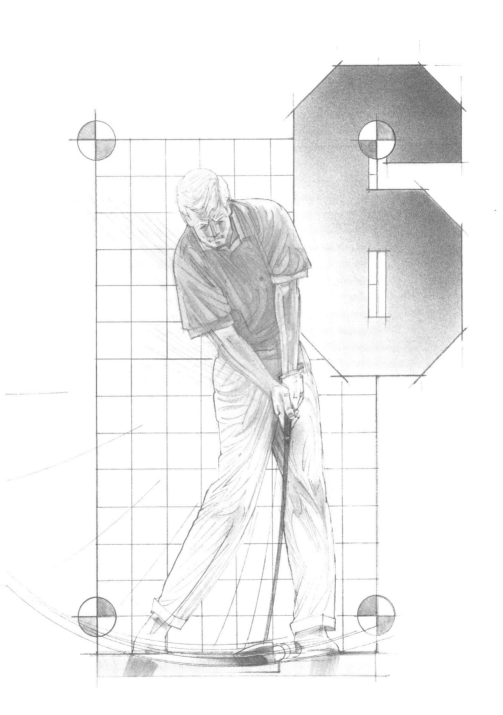

STEP 6

# STEP 6

# IMPACT

You should know by now that impact might not be the moment of truth, but it's still massively important. We know that the hands-and-arms golfer, the senior golfer, the thick-chested golfer, and golfers with limited mobility will have less hip rotation. We know that the golfer with an open clubface at the top of backswing will use more hands at impact, although open-clubface players sometimes bow the left wrist (top-hand wrist) starting down to square the clubface. A supple, younger golfer with great transition at Step 5a will have more hip rotation and shoulder rotation at impact, which will give them less need for wrist action but more speed.

Rotation is a multiplier for speed. Knowing all of this, I look for correct impact alignments within proven safety zones. The handsy golfer and the less-rotational golfer will have the hips nearly square at impact. The closed-clubface golfer will have more hip rotation, up to 70 degrees open at impact. Therefore, the corridor of success, the safety zone for hip rotation, is very wide and depends on a number of things such as age, flexibility, leg action, and clubface orientation at Step 5a (the real moment of truth).

Here's what I'd like to see from a golfer at impact:

1. The lead wrist is flat or bowed when swinging an iron.
2. The shaft is leaning toward the target.

3. The club should be delofted.
4. The trail-hand wrist should be bent away from the target.
5. The bottom of the swing should be ahead of the ball.

**Supination** is the term we use for rotating the lead arm in the downswing to square the clubface. To get a feeling for this rotation, I have people place their lead hand flat on a table (palm down). Then I tell them to turn the hand completely over, so the knuckles are touching the table. I explain how the radial bone in the lead arm is responsible for the rotation that squares the clubface—not the wrist. All good golf swings have supination.

## STEP 6 HEAD POSITION

My research shows that most top players will lower their head slightly during the downswing from the position it was in at address. Most tour players also will also return the head close to the address position, but back for a driver and down for an iron. The shoulders will be rounded. The lowering of the head surprises many golfers when they see it on video. The truth is, the more lag you employ in the swing, the more the head lowers.

Lateral movement of the hips and knees will create a longer and thinner divot. Your belt, or center of your core, should move three to seven inches forward by impact when hitting a quality iron shot. When you're swinging a driver, the head moves differently. Because the ball is teed up, you hit off a flat piece of turf, the driver is your flattest club, you're standing the farthest from the ball of any club, and you should strike the ball with a level or ascending blow, the head should move away from the target by impact. It should never drift toward the target.

Keegan Bradley at impact.

## THE LEAD ELBOW OUTWARD

I was taught by Carl Welty that coming into impact and at impact, the lead elbow points somewhat at the target. That means the forearm has internally rotated. So in my teaching, I've always looked at how the lead arm moved to impact. This is why many great players have the lead arm bent coming down to impact. Most teachers and golfers see this as a mistake. I've had students beg me to fix the bend in the lead arm. But look at Cristie Kerr, one of my early students who played top world-class golf with a bent left elbow!

Lenny Mattiace told me that the best ball-striker he ever saw was Retief Goosen (two-time U.S. Open champion). Retief has a major bend in the lead elbow. Same with Rickie Fowler and many other great players. Most teachers don't know that many great ball-strikers have some bend in the elbow. Carl showed me many examples of tour players with the elbow pointing at the target. Jordan Spieth carries the bent elbow past impact into a position we term "the chicken wing." It's highly unusual to see a top player chicken wing on a full out golf swing, but it has certainly worked for Jordan. I define him as the ultimate drag-style swinger. The problem with dragging is diminished power, but the benefit is the ability to keep the clubface square for a longer period of time. You will see tour players chicken wing some punch shots or short pitch shots on TV. The players with the bent lead elbow coming down normally straighten out the arm into the extension position (Step 7b).

That straightening is a second lever for power. The lesson here is, a bent elbow in your lead arm coming down is not a mistake. Many great golf champions have bend in the lead arm.

Hitting up on a driver while maintaining a strong lead wrist.

Rory McIlroy at impact. The lead side is going vertical. You can see the club hitting up, well off the ground and the ball is visible near his left leg. Notice how the clubface is released.

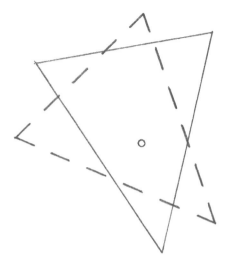

This seemingly crazy image of two triangles can be explained. The solid triangle represents your set up position (the shoulders and arms). The dotted triangle represents the position of the triangle just past impact at 7a. You do not return the upper body to the original position. Far from it.

Pro impact shows the hands forward of the head and the fundamental flat lead wrist. Notice the angle of his belt.

## THE MYSTERY OF THE LEFT FOOT AT IMPACT
## (HEEL OFF THE GROUND)

### Pro Example: Lexi Thompson

There is a great deal of confusion concerning what the lead foot (left for right-handers) should be doing as the club reaches the ball. I got caught up in the controversy when I was teaching Lexi Thompson, then a young teenager. Nothing was said until after she won the U.S. Junior Amateur at age thirteen and was playing successfully in LPGA Tour events the following year. That's when some commentator noticed that Lexi comes off her lead heel at impact. I'm guessing those who found fault were obviously not aware that a young Tiger Woods's lead foot did the same thing. And they probably didn't know that Johnny Miller and Bobby Jones came off their left heel too. These are a few examples of players who used this common leverage move. Currently, 20 percent of PGA TOUR players let their left foot come off the ground, including major champs Louis Oosthuizen, Bubba Watson, and Justin Thomas.

When Lexi was very young, her dad, Scott, asked me about her lead foot moving, because a number of teachers told him this was a bad thing. They said her technique was wrong and had to change or she would never be good. Scott was concerned but knew most teachers really didn't understand leverage or how some people use the ground to generate more power. I explained that we wouldn't change this aspect of Lexi's golf swing, and that by elevating her left leg and left side, she was achieving more power. The result today is that she is the best driver and top ball-striker on the LPGA Tour. I'm sure nearly every female professional player on the planet would immediately trade swings with her.

169

Lexi Thompson goes airborne at impact, just as she did at twelve years old. It's a power move and I never took it away. Both heels off the ground. I knew Bobby Jones and other greats who did the same.

It's so important to know what should be changed in a golf swing and what should be left to the individual. This book will help you make those determinations for your own swing. What a shame it would be to take something out of your swing and then learn some of golf's greatest players do exactly the same thing. I'll add that another great young talent, Justin Thomas, has the exact left-foot movement as Lexi Thompson.

## Explanation

The power move discussed above is up and into the lead toe in the impact zone, and then back away from the target. Even though the great Bobby Jones came up on his toes at impact back in the 1920s, apparently everyone missed this. As previously noted in our tour studies, we have always noticed that at least 20 percent of PGA TOUR players are up on the toes at impact. Bubba Watson, who has been a leader in greens in regulation and one of the greatest drivers I've ever seen (super long and straight), has had his lead foot slide a huge amount back and away from the target. This is because the lead hip stops its forward motion and reverses direction. This creates an extremely powerful force.

Is there lateral motion? Yes. It's not pure hip rotation from the top. The lead knee (left) flexes forward in transition and always ahead of the hip. Weight moves to the lead side in transition, not away. You get to the lead side first, and then the hip pulls away. On BodiTrak, which measures vertical force, the trace is called the Z trace. There is a sequence to this power move.

Justin Thomas, Lexi Thompson, Gary Woodland, Bubba Watson, and other power players will have more pressure in the trail foot at impact with a driver. This is a move more and more teachers are passing on to students. I wrote extensively about this in *The Complete Hogan,* published in 2012. You can also look at the illustration in this book from *The X-Factor Swing,* where I show weight pushing down with the right foot, forcing the body to stay more centered and not sliding ahead of the ball. The Z trace shows a segmented shift, first forward then back for a split second with some tour players like Justin Thomas.

## Pro Example: Gary Woodland

I'm demonstrating impact alignments to a golf school. These types of visuals have an "aha moment" for many students.

When Gary Woodland came to work with me in 2015, he wanted to get back to hitting a fade—especially with his driver. So I started at Step 6, checking his impact alignments and his contact point on the clubface. Before coming to work with me, he had been playing a draw, so I knew it would not be easy to get him to fade it routinely in competition—at least not right away. The very first thing I did was utilize clubface tape. I do this with all my students. It's important to know where the clubface is meeting the ball. With Gary, sure enough, every driver swing resulted in a slight toe strike—meaning that if you were looking at his clubface, you'd see an impact mark just left of center—the side farthest from the hosel. Gary hit at least forty drivers that day, and they were all on the toe side. When that happens, something called the gear effect takes place.

The clubface opens upon contact and causes ball to rotate in the opposite direction—like two gears—and that puts hook spin on the shot. The driver's face is designed so that it's only flat in the center. The ends are curved (*bulge-and-roll* is the term for this design) to somewhat correct off-center hits. Because Gary was hooking his tee shots, I knew one way to get him to hit a fade was having him move impact to the center of the clubface. This is fundamental in ball-striking.

When I used a TrackMan launch monitor to analyze Gary's swing, I was surprised to find he was hitting 5 to 6 degrees down on the ball with his driver. That's very unusual for a top-class player, especially someone who can routinely hit drives in excess of three hundred yards. By hitting down on the ball, combined with a swing path that was inside-out, his launch angle was too low (9 to 10 degrees). I carefully studied the video to confirm his swing path and his body rotation in the impact zone. When I correctly diagnosed his problem, it was time to start teaching. Over decades of work, I have accumulated a massive number of ways to explain, demonstrate, and teach the alignments at impact. All students are different, and as a teacher, you must have many ways to help each golfer.

Gary Woodland is a top athlete and is capable of doing many things quickly; however, changing his swing path and angle of attack so that he could hit a power fade with a better trajectory took some time. Gary loved what we were working on so much, after just a few weeks he moved to Miami to be near my teaching headquarters at the Doral Resort. Over a span of about a month, I helped him change his path by 3 or 4 degrees, and his angle of attack to near 0 degrees. Those are big changes, and I knew it would take time until he would be comfortable with them—especially on a Sunday afternoon in a PGA TOUR event when money and status are on the line. Making centerface contact was the easiest adjustment. It went hand in hand with our work on Track-Man. I adjusted his setup to be more open and had him stand about an inch closer to the ball. Getting any golfer to stand the correct distance from the ball and have the ball played in the correct location in relation to the body are paramount to hitting it in the center of the clubface. Gary hit it best with the ball played off his left instep. He also used a forward press, moving his left hip up and forward just before he took the club away. I also had him turn his left toe slightly outward to increase hip rotation in the downswing.

Gary had a weak grip, meaning his left thumb was resting more on top of the handle, and we kept that position to accommodate a wrist injury, not to mention it helped him hit some of the longest drives on tour. The weak grip help set the club toe down at the top of his backswing.

We focused on centerface contact, swinging the club more up on the ball and left after impact. It was not long before his angle of attack was 0 (meaning perfectly level) and sometimes 1 degree up. Also, his launch angle was now 12 degrees, which enabled him to carry the ball even farther than he already did. With those adjustments, the driver shots he hit were just incredible. His swing speed has always been fast, but with the path and angle of attack adjustments, it increased to 126 miles per hour. The tour average is around 113. When he practiced at Doral, the newly lengthened driving range was not long enough for his biggest drives.

I'm proud of the work we did during those eighteen months in 2015 and 2016. Gary Woodland was so great to work with. By improving his setup and putting our emphasis on Step 6 (impact), Gary got that power fade. I went to quite a few tournaments with him and saw him strike the ball at the highest professional level. By the end of the 2015, it was really good. In

2016, his driving was even better. In 2015, he lost the finals of the WGC Match Play championship to Rory McIlroy. For much of that year, Gary had injury and health issues.

At the U.S. Open, I walked a practice round with him and Dustin Johnson. It was an incredible driving exhibition from both of them. They agreed that Chambers Bay, site of the Open that year, was a course they could score on, because they could fly most of the bunkers. Gary and Dustin played great that day and Dustin would go on to finish second to Jordan Spieth. Unfortunately, Gary picked up a strange virus and got very sick. He ended up in the hospital, missed the practice rounds, and eventually missed the cut. I would have liked to see what he could have done if he was healthy that week. I'm sure it would have been great. Before flying into Seattle that week for the Open, Gary had shot a 59 back in Kansas and a 61 at Dismal Bay in Nebraska, breaking the course record there by seven shots.

I was extremely excited to see Gary Woodland win the 2019 U.S. Open and fulfill his huge potential. Gary has worked with some top teachers in our game and coaches in other sports. Gary has been super diligent in attaining the best possible information. Besides his huge success in golf, Gary is also one of the best guys on tour and one of the most generous to the Folds of Honor and other charities.

## Summary

The lesson for you is that getting into a good impact position starts at setup. Checking your impact alignments are critical for ball-striking improvement. Go through the checklist for Step 6 to identify where you can improve. Understand that impact is one of the key positions that all top professional golfers work on constantly.

# THE JAKE DRILL

The Jake Drill. It's one of my favorites, invented for PGA TOUR player Peter Jacobsen. Famous caddie Fluff Cowan would hold a headcover when Peter was at tour events. This is one way I train students to keep the arms in and stop inward extension of the body. Plus a good shaft return.

Returning to my work with tour professional Peter Jacobsen, I used this Step 6 drill. I would hold a shaft just above where I wanted his golf club to be at impact. His job was to swing and miss the shaft, which forced him to stay in his golf posture longer into the through-swing. I did this to fix his bad habit of rising out of his address posture too soon and having the shaft rise too steep. He loved the feeling this drill created of returning the shaft closer to his body and closer to where it started. His caddie at that time, Fluff Cowen, began holding a driver with a headcover on it in front of Peter as he practiced. Peter used this drill nonstop on the PGA TOUR, so I named it the "Jake Drill" in my *Golf Digest Book of Drills*. (Jake is his nickname.)

## SQUARING THE CLUBFACE

### Inward Pull and Outward Push

Think of your lead arm as the one that drags or pulls the club through impact. The left hand is on top of the grip, and thus moves on what I call the inward circle as you swing the club. To comprehend this idea, mimic a golf swing without a club from address to impact, paying attention to the circle-like motion being made with the left hand. When you swing the club with just your lead arm, you will feel pull. That's the inner-circle hand path. The right hand is lower on the grip and traces the outward path at the same time. The right hand is farthest away from your lower center of mass and can be thought of as the throwing arm.

To square the clubface, there should be an equal amount of inward pull and outward throw. Too much pull would leave the face open, while too much push would close the face. Many amateur golfers make an early throw in the downswing, meaning they use too much trail arm and trail hand as they swing toward the ball. The trail arm straightens too soon, and the club whips past the hands. This early release causes deceleration, an outside-in swing path, and a huge loss of power.

Occasionally, I'll see the opposite—golfers with too much pull. They're usually better players. They're lagging the clubhead excessively and have too much shaft lean at impact. This usually produces shots that are too low and miss right of the target. To correct this flaw, the golfer uses a late flipping action of the hands to square the face. Any golfer who has had to rely on trying to save the shot with his or her hands knows it's not a reliable way to swing. It's an awful feeling that does not produce consistent ball-striking. All advanced golfers know exactly what I'm saying. Sometimes too much lag, followed by this late hand action in the downswing, is referred to as "dragging and flipping."

That's why you need a balance of push and pull to get the best ball-striking results. I'll teach a golfer to swing with more or less lag depending on whether I see them pushing or pulling too much. Each student must be assessed individually. Sometimes there is more drag and other times there is pull. If you understand impact and the allowable safety zones, you can work your golf swing back from Step 6 (impact). Position teaching like this is so helpful to golfers who are lost about how to swing a club. It's very hard to do something if you don't see it clearly or understand it physically. We use TrackMan and launch monitors so our students can see all impact alignments. Many times I will have to teach an exaggerated feel until the student is successful; they think they have made a big swing change. Almost always they have not done enough. I'll tell them we need more.

I teach miniswings to my students. This drill produces width and excellent swing direction.

Here's is a concept using push or pull: watch your hands as you begin the backswing. The top hand starts on an inside rail and the lower hand moves on the outside rail. When you do this, the club stays in front of the chest.

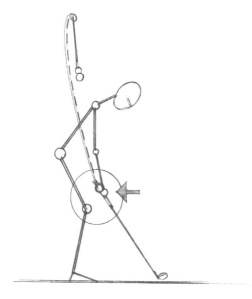

A look at hand path up and down. For most top ball-strikers the hands come down slightly outside of the backswing path. The shaft works the opposite by falling later (shallowing).

It's quite possible to have the lead hand (left for right-handers) pull out and away from the body, shifting your left hand onto the outside rail. That's too much pull with the hands moving over the plane. The right hand should be on that outside rail coming to impact. When the left hand moves to the outside, it indicates too much pull in the swing leading to deep divots, low shots, shanking, or that flipping move with the hands. So pay attention to what rail the left and right hand are moving on. I know this can be confusing and might require reading several times. I give credit to Jimmy Ballard for this concept. Jimmy spent a lot of time with me, and I learned so much from his amazing teaching.

**IMPACT**

## THE RELEASE

My friend Andy Brumer is a terrific golf writer, and he implored me to talk more about the release. He correctly stated that when throwing a ball, the release doesn't occur until you actually let go of the ball. It's that concept of letting go that we usually identify with the word *release*. In golf, you're not letting go of the club physically when you release it. Yet, that term *release* is one of the most important in the golf swing.

I played many times with the great Canadian golfer Moe Norman. He is regarded by many as one of the best ball-strikers of all time. Moe always said the key to his swing was "letting go!" I can't tell you how many times I've used those words to my students. And not just about physically swinging the club. We let go mentally to play great golf too.

How should you release the club and let it go? It's more than just using your hands to let the clubhead release. Jimmy Ballard, who taught more tour pros at one time than anyone in the history of golf instruction, said you release the entire right side. That's a great definition.

I've written about the two opposing releases in golf, with one being the *block* or *drag release* and the other being the *early* or *throw release*. In this description, I'm only talking about the arm, hand, and wrist action. However, you should remember that the entire right side also should be releasing, just like Jimmy said. A slower body rotation will require an earlier release of the arms and hands (a throw). A fast body will allow for a late release, or what I call the drag release.

A top-ball striker certainly has a constantly increasing driving force into and past impact. It's true that the clubhead slows down slightly before impact, but good players try to keep their swing speed up past impact. We call it "hitting through the ball." Upon impact, the club will slow down, but this decrease in speed

180

is far more jarring in amateur swings. When a golfer contacts the ball, the club slows until separation. A poor golf swing will slow down by 50 percent or more, but a top ball-striker's swing will slow only a fraction of that. I think every top ball-striker has the distinct feeling of not slowing down. I believe that means the release happens after the ball springs off the clubface, just like when a pitcher lets go of the ball.

## DRILL: RIGHT-ARM-ONLY

One of our staple drills done at every golf school is learning a correct right arm swing. Actually, almost everybody learns the

feeling of a correct throw release, a great way to loosen up stiff swings. Using a short iron is best, and tee up the ball, but first make at least ten practice swings where you go for a nice Step 8 finish. There should be minimal tension, lots of freedom, and the sense of how the hands and arms work in a full release.

## DRILL: PINCH THE DIME (JIMMY BALLARD)

When a golfer coils into the brace of the right leg and then drives off the inside of the right foot, this springing action of the legs tightens all the muscles of the inside of the legs up through the posterior back. Imagine, just prior to initiating the change of direction with the kick of the right foot and right knee, that you had a dime "where the sun don't shine"—that is, between the

Pinching the dime. Glutes squeezed.

182

cheeks of your buttocks. During the entire releasing action clear to finish, hold the dime. This was written in 1981 and describes the vertical force of the body. This description is something anyone can understand and something that I see in all modern power drivers.

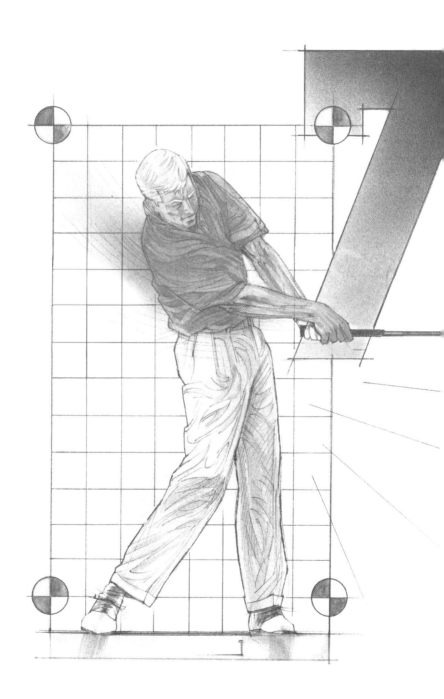

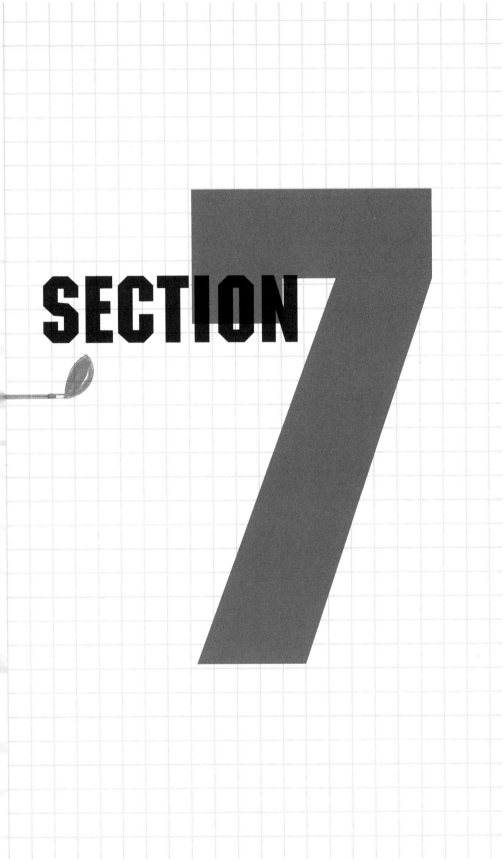

SECTION 7

# STEP 7A

# POSTIMPACT

Three feet past impact is another underappreciated position in the swing. In truth, the more sophisticated the golfer, the easier it is for that person to understand and implement additional steps. Since I teach students on every level, I still often spend time on this postimpact position, mostly through half-swing drills and holding the Step 7a position to feel the resistance required through impact.

Here's what to look for when watching from the down-the-line (DL) and face-on (FO) perspectives for Step 7a:

DL: The shaft is pointing at the target line. Notice I said *pointed* at the target line. That means the clubhead and shaft are pointed at the target line. Many golfers think the clubhead should be on the line or even to the right of the line. It's a big eye-opener.

DL: The clubface is square to the plane. This means the toe of the clubhead is in front of the heel. I want to see the right arm on top of the left.

FO: The hips rise (vertical action).

FO: The lead leg has moved laterally past its location at address.

FO: The lead shoulder is rising and rotating.

FO: The hands are moving upward, and the club's shaft appears between the arms.

FO: The clubshaft is forward of the setup position.

Step 7a, postimpact when the club is three feet past impact. The shaft points between the arms. The toe of the club is released.

## Pro Example: Bo Hoag

Bo was an All-American at Ohio State and is currently working on his odyssey of making it to the PGA TOUR. He's a great example of someone who worked hard to improve Step 7 (release) and had excellent results. I started working with Bo when he was twenty-eight and didn't have any status on the big pro tours. One of the first things I noticed was his position at Step 7a. Bo held off the clubhead from squaring and pulled his arms inward. The clubhead's orientation was well to the right of the ideal position I'm looking for in Step 7b. But the root of the problem started post-impact at Step 7a. Whenever a golfer routinely hits blocks or hooks—as was Bo's issue—I'll have them study video of great swings. I'll show them how the clubface should look and where the shaft should be at that point in the swing.

Even in a small pitch drill we see great 7a fundamentals. The lead side is up, the shaft points between the arms, and the clubface is square.

Dustin Johnson is able to move the hands far forward at impact due to the closed clubface coming down, as well as his bowed wrist at the top. Keegan Bradley is in the background.

*The great Sir Nick Faldo at a perfect 7a position.*

Once Bo understood this and knew how to correct his issue, he started practicing Step 7a and the results were immediate. I had Bo get to this position using a variety of clubs, and he really got it locked in. As I suspected, focusing on the release also helped Bo with his downswing. He tended to drop the arms behind him starting down (from Step 4 to Step 5a). But by working on the leftward movement of the club at Step 7a, that drop-behind move in his transition started to vanish. Bo had to qualify for the Web.com Tour, which is very difficult to do, but he made the cut in twelve of thirteen tournaments. In 2018, he was fully exempt on the Web.com, and while this book was in production, he qualified for the 2020 PGA TOUR. He won the first Korn Ferry tour event in Portland, Oregon, shooting 22 under.

Bo's problem at Step 7a was driving the clubhead too far down the line with an open face. Like all of my students, I wanted him to understand what he was doing wrong and how to correct it. It helps to show photos and videos to reinforce these ideas, then drills can help the player feel the correct movement. Finally, I'll have them implement the new move in real time. This is all part of my teaching system, and all my teachers are trained to follow these steps.

In Bo's case, I asked him to describe what this new release pattern felt like. Once he described it, I was able to devise a drill that matched his description of the change. I do this to keep students engaged and make them feel like they're taking part in creating the solution to the swing flaw. Although I'm guiding them, the student is participating like a second teacher.

## DRILL

Bo likes to focus on what the left arm is doing to make his swing better, so I gave him a feel involving the left thumbnail. I showed him how he could prevent the clubface from being open by focusing on keeping the nail on his left thumb cocked downward and turning left past impact.

The goal is to slowly turn the left thumbnail past impact (Bo was not rotating the wrist), which makes the clubshaft move the same way on the arc. Bo did this drill with his left arm only hundreds of times. His ball-striking dramatically improved.

191

STEP 7B

# STEP 7B

# EXTENSION POSITION

The extension position is something all of us at JMGS teach incessantly to our students. Nothing looks worse than the crumpled up arms at Step 7b, the infamous chicken wing. My students would like to throw up when they see themselves on video with the terrible look of poor extension.

The cause of poor extension comes from numerous death moves that happen before we get to 7b. Here's the teaching trick we use at JMGS: I carefully put my students in a good impact position, in the postimpact, and then in 7b. I have them hold each position. I also show them what good extension looks like. See the pro picture on the following page.

A part of not being able to execute a key golf position is not clearly visualizing it, so study the details of the picture. Do you see the right foot? It's rolling off the instep. You can copy this.

Do you see the transfer of weight to the left side? Do you see that the belt buckle is the closet part of the pro's body to the target? Now look at the arms. For many students, this is the most important thing to learn. The right arm is fully extended and straight. The left arm is still connected to the body and is straight or close to straight.

Now look at the shoulders and notice how high the left shoulder is and see that the right shoulder is well under. The pro's head is beginning to release. His eyes are already picking up the

Keegan Bradley at extension position. I teach this position relentlessly. Phil Mickelson is watching. I'm standing with Butch Harmon.

flight of the ball. The clubshaft is parallel to the target line. I suggest lots of mirror work copying the positions and of course checking your positions prior to extension. This is how the entire golf swing falls into place. Every top ball-striker is great through the extension position.

## Pro Example: Vaughn Taylor

During Vaughn Taylor's long PGA TOUR career, I've worked with him at numerous times. Our last session was at Doral in 2016, and he won the very next week at the AT&T Pebble Beach National Pro-Am. One of the things we worked on was the extension position after impact (Step 7b). Vaughn has a beautiful, graceful golf swing that has earned him a place on a U.S. Ryder Cup team. But his hip rotation through impact will sometimes get too slow; then the arms race ahead. This would get Vaughn out of sync, and his swing would become unreliable. So we focused our most recent work on Step 7b. I had Vaughn simulate the extension position of great ball-strikers below.

194

It's very important to study this drawing and to particularly note the position of the right wrist.

*Notice the right wrist is extended downwards (ulnar deviation). The right thumb is down.*

It's fully cocked downward, which means the fingers of the right hand are as low as possible and under the right forearm. Also notice that the right arm is fully extended and the shaft is in a straight line with the right arm. I had Vaughn make easy swings, stopping the movement at this point. If you've never tried this, you probably don't realize how difficult it is to stop the club at this point in the swing. Because of this, I had Vaughn hit 7-iron shots only eighty yards. He gradually swung faster and faster, eventually hitting that club nearly its normal distance. But each time he would stop halfway into the follow-through. The left wrist cannot be seen in the illustration above, but it's important to note what it's doing. The left wrist is not bowed; instead, it's just slightly cupped and the left thumbnail is facing down. This release produces a straight, low bullet shot. If you keep the left wrist bowed, the ball will usually go to the right of

**EXTENSION POSITION**

the target. The release I'm describing, the one I taught Vaughn, is a perfect, top-class pro release. It's a release that produces tremendous compression.

Look at the left arm and shoulder in the illustration of Vaugh below. The left shoulder is high, and the right shoulder is low. I measured the angle at 45 degrees. The left arm is straight, but not disconnected. That means the upper part of the left arm is

Upper triangle has released in front of Vaughn Taylor's chest. His right knee has kicked out toward the target line.

still connected to the top of the left side of the torso. Meanwhile, the right arm has gone from slightly bent at impact (Step 6) to straight at Step 7b. You could say Vaughn's practice with the 7 iron was solely done for improving Step 7. I prefer to think of it as a drill that gets you to move from a great impact position to the perfect extension position. In my golf schools, we teach this extension position to everyone. A top professional like Vaughn can really improve Step 7b in a short amount of time and then go out and win with it. But for most of you, it will take diligence and a good deal of practice to hone Step 7b. It's probably the toughest step for students to replicate when they swing.

Looking from the ground up, notice how Vaughn has rolled off the right instep, and the right heel is not that high off the turf. I teach that footwork to everybody. The right knee has kicked forward and outward toward the ball. Also, notice that the left leg and hip pocket can be seen. That flexion in the right knee is one key to staying down and in your spine angle past impact. This indicates there was good rotation of the pelvis. Filming a driver swing down the target line, it's important to see the hands from this viewpoint. In the illustration on the previous page, the hands don't disappear in front of the body. If they did, it would mean they moved too far to the left of the target line. However, both the hands and club will disappear at the next instant of the golf swing.

Other things to note: the golf shaft is parallel to the target line, and Vaughn's head has swiveled so his eyes can immediately pick up the ball's flight. I check to see if the entire right side of the body has released at Step 7b. Stopping the club at Step 7b is a great drill, one you can practice in a mirror at home or at the driving range.

## STEP 7B DOWN THE LINE

In 2006, I produced a DVD, *The Powerline*. I first sold each DVD for $1,000, then I raised the price to $1,250. It took so many years of research to produce that selling it for $19.95 was unthinkable. I spent those years reviewing videotape and finally discovering the power release used by the greats of the game. I'm talking about the movement of the shaft and clubhead from halfway down in the swing (Step 5b) to halfway into the follow-through (Step 7b). The DVD highlighted startling similarities in how pros moved from Step 5b to Step 7a. I called it the "powerline" because the alignments matched up.

Remember that filming the correct way every time is essential to the research. You might be surprised by some of the top teachers who bought that DVD. Of course, most top teachers know a lot more about the release and the positions now, fourteen years later. That video definitely had something to do with the power leap forward in the swing.

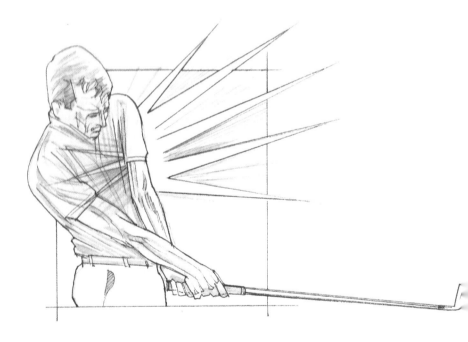

*Jammed and overconnected, poor extension, filled with tension.*

**BUILD YOUR SWING**

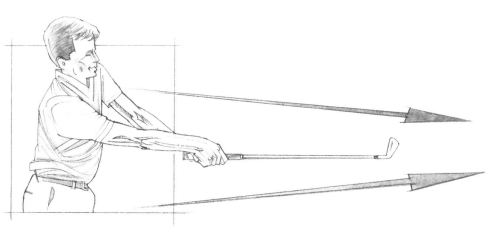

Overextended.

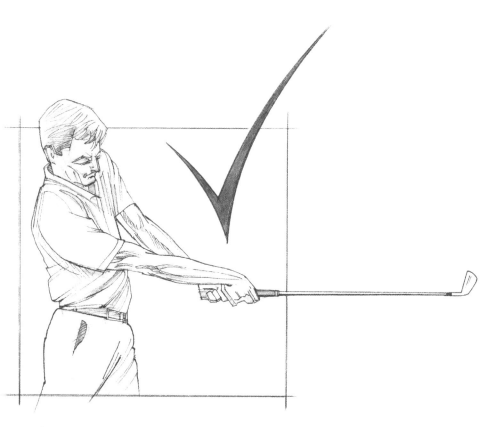

Correct extension. Make sure to practice correctly.

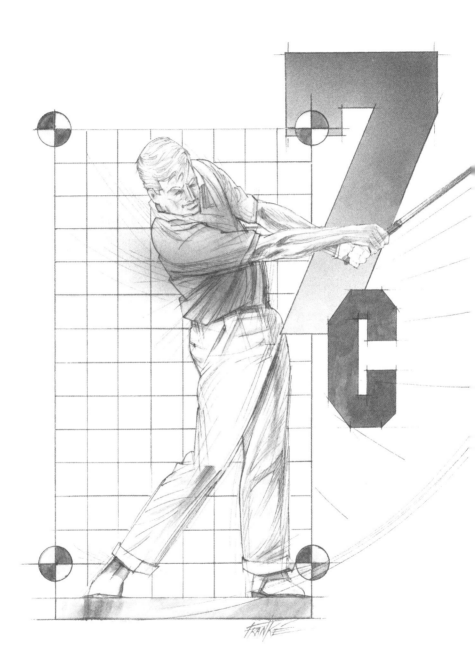

# STEP 7C
# THE SCISSOR EFFECT

I wrote an article decades ago that deserves an update. It's about how a golf ball flies off the face of the club just as the clubshaft diverges on the inclined shaft plane far left of the ball in flight (right-handed golfer). I was mesmerized by the amazing view the camera showed down the target line just after impact. I called it the "scissor effect" as in opening a pair of scissors with one blade opening away from the straight blade. It's what I see when the club goes left after impact while the ball whistles straight down the target line.

I must have watched the top professionals on videotape a million times from perfect angles. I watched a friend, PGA TOUR pro Jim Simons, hundreds of times from down the target line the in the late 1970s, and thousands thereafter. I also took lots of video from the 45-degree angle out in front of other tour players that shows this idea perfectly.

A clear example of the scissor effect came from research with four-time PGA TOUR winner Jim Simons. Jim was my first-year roommate and best friend at the University of Houston. We played together all the time at Houston and continued to play together in amateur events, U.S. Amateur practice rounds, and U.S. Open practice rounds. Jim and I would discuss everything about the golf swing. I had perfect down-the-line video of Si-

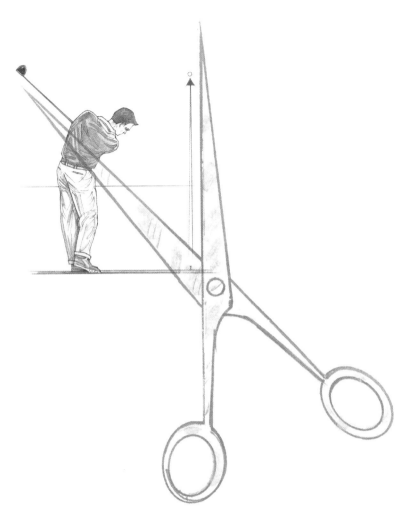

Clubhead and clubshaft go left while the ball goes straight at the target.

mons when he won a PGA TOUR event. I watched it over and over, comparing it to all the other great professional golfers.

I saw the club shaft swinging immediately up the shaft plane to the left on the forward swing while the golf ball ripped down the target line. It took a very diverse takeoff from where the club-head went and obviously to the orbit of the clubhead. I had the distinct feeling it was very much like opening a pair of scissors. The club opens like a pair of scissors or swings to the left (for the right-handed golfer) and the ball goes straight down the line. It was my study of Jim Simons that really opened my eyes to something I had not completely understood as a young teacher.

At Step 7c, the club has been released right up the plane just under the lead shoulder.

The player moves up and through to a tall finish in perfect balance, no strain on the lower back. After holding the full finish position, the player spins the shaft down to rebound (Step 8).

The scissor effect: Sergio Garcia shows the exit plane, Step 7c. Clubshaft is left and ball flies away to the right and at the target.

## THE RIGHT-ARM CROSS: THE RED DOT

The right-arm cross is something I've also taught for decades because of the scissors observations. I've used a red dot placed strategically in my indoor Superstation bay, which I first started using at Sunningdale Country club in New York (my first head pro job). Later, I would do the same at Quaker Ridge, Tamarisk, Sleepy Hollow, Doral, and now after my latest move to the Biltmore Hotel in Coral Gables, Florida. This dot is placed so my students can specifically see the leftward plane of the shaft early after impact. Going through the ball, I watched how great players crossed their chests with the right arm, which combined with the club shaft, formed the opening of the scissors. So, a main teaching idea is that you want that right arm in tight and crossing the torso. It's across the body and under the shoulder plane in this section of the swing. It's definitely a different feeling for the golfer trying for either the high finish or trying to swing the club too far down the target line.

Two poor ideas for most golfers can be trying for an overly "high finish" or the concept of driving the trail arm down the target line. But in high-level golf, the right arm should work on a plane and point at my red dot. I've taught this idea to major champions on the pro tours and many other tour winners. All my students know the red dot!

Johnny Miller's shaft would point at my red dot. Notice the weight on his left heel and left hip back.

**THE SCISSOR EFFECT**

## Pro Example: Tom Kite

Tom Kite and I began working full time in 1992. One of the main issues was an inside-out swing path. We started in January at La Costa. I came up with all kinds of drills to stop this. One was to hit balls against a board faced down the target line. Another was to start the ball left of his target line. We did this all the time, including at my Florida home where Tom hit a ball through the net in my in-room video studio and buried it in my wall. The ball actually stuck in the wall behind the net. I left it there until the day I sold the house. Tom Kite won the U.S. Open that year at Pebble Beach (1992).

Visualize a chain attached to a wall. See the illustration on page 211. Pull that chain out of the wall level left. Your body leads and the arm stays connected to the body. The hand goes around.

The action of the club and shaft through the impact zone has always been a focal point of my teaching and my talks around the world. It led me to write an editorial in *PGA Magazine* in 1989 about the incorrect way the PGA had been teaching ball-flight laws. It was not an easy sell because, at that time, path was considered the king of starting direction, and there were nine possible ball flights based on that assumption. I knew it was wrong back then, but it has really taken TrackMan launch monitors to convince teachers and golfers alike that *clubface is king*.

I have one last story on the scissors and ball flight. It involves the great Davis Love III and an opposite view. It happened in 1994. Davis would often practice down at my side of the range during the Doral PGA TOUR event. He would be down there usually with Faxon and Kite. One day I asked Davis which way the ball started and why? I asked this question because I knew Davis would likely answer it wrong. He said the ball started on swing path. I then hit some small shots with the club first closed, and then open, showing clearly that the ball started on the angle of the face when hit easily. He just smiled, shook his head, and said he didn't know that.

The thing to note here is that great players have been told things that might not be true, yet they instinctively do the correct motion anyway. Lots of great players think *path*. So if you have that natural scissor effect, it doesn't matter what you're thinking. Davis Love is a great player and great players often think much less than many teachers know. They just hit a golf ball. They are extremely gifted. They have a feel for the game. If something doesn't need to be fixed, don't fix it.

## STEP 7C SHAFT EXIT

I wrote an article in *Golf Illustrated* entitled "Swing Left to Swing Right" in 1989. It came from my research and understanding of the swing plane, only it was about the front side of the swing. It is still an undertaught part of the golf swing. You see the exit

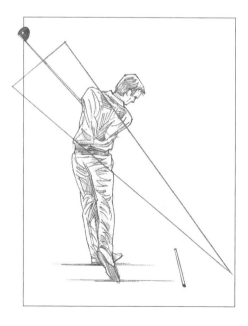

The shaft exits within the safety zone.

plane looking down the line. I knew from playing with great players, especially in Texas, that the golf club swung way more left than most golfers understood. This especially true for fades or lower ball flight. I started looking at where the shaft appeared through the body. It is not exactly the same for all greats, but it's in a safety zone. Like most things in golf, there is a safety zone.

## The Scissor Effect

In a professional golf swing, looking down the target line, the shaft exits very close to the shoulder plane. You see the shaft appear without the arms.

The higher the exit, the higher the shot trajectory. It also favors a draw. The lower exit indicates a low trajectory and favors a fade.

Lexi Thompson shows the scissor effect. Her golf club has swung left, under her hands, while the golf ball is tangent, on another line (ripping straight down the fairway).

## 7c Body Angles (Down the Line)

It is so important to check the shoulder angle at Step 7c. The right shoulder is down, while the left shoulder has elevated to its highest point. The shaft and the shoulders will come close to the magic 45-degree angle.

The spine will be at a deep angle with the shaft sometimes forming a line close to a 90-degree angle. Of course, these angles are not easy to simulate for older golfers or golfers with injuries.

Video certainly comes in handy when showing students their positions, and how and where we need to make improvements.

A vertical, or steep, shaft position at this stage of the swing is very common. It indicates improper leverage of the hands and

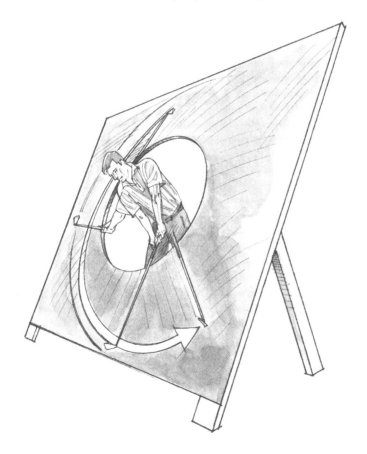

arms in an effort to swing the club down the line. Students are surprised when I draw an arc on the ground to explain clubhead path. There is no line to the target, but rather an arc action. Through impact, the shaft must work back up the shaft plane. Again, a huge revelation to so many.

## EXIT PLANE

### Pro Example: Lexi Thompson

Lexi Thompson started coming to my golf school when she was eight. While I oversaw her progress with my teaching staff, I really started working one-on-one with her when she was twelve. At that time, she had a super strong grip and a vertical release, but she could still win tournaments.

Her shaft would exit through her head. Lexi had a short backswing and a huge hook. We started working on that grip and on her swing plane past impact. To be honest, we worked on this aspect of her swing through all the years we worked, until she was eighteen. It was an issue that sometimes would return. This problem caused her to fight a block to the right or a hard hook. As she got stronger and bigger, I knew it would get to be a huge problem unless she also corrected that grip. I did all kinds of swing exercises with her and used images of great players to improve this aspect of her swing. One of our main swing exercises was to hit short irons with a cut-off finish.

This short finish would stop the club on the exit plane. Believe me, this took a lot of work. I also showed Lexi tons of Lee Trevino wedge swings to improve her move to 7c. She had an issue of staying too far under the plane and getting inside out on the downswing. When we got this corrected, she won everything as a junior and went directly to the LPGA Tour at eighteen. She won the U.S. Junior at thirteen and made the U.S. Curtis Cup Team when she was fourteen, a record that might not ever be broken. Lexi also qualified for every U.S. Open since age twelve. She won a major at age nineteen!

She almost won an LPGA event at age fourteen, and she was the No. 1-ranked junior and amateur. At the same time Lexi finished tenth at the U.S. Open when she was fifteen and won an LPGA event at age sixteen. She's been ranked as high as No. 2 in the world. There is usually one or two swing issues we all naturally have that come back from time to time. When that steep exit angle returns for Lexi, she knows exactly what to work on in practice. She is definitely one of the best ball-strikers in women's golf.

## PULL-THE-CHAIN DRILL

Extend your left arm out parallel to the ground with the thumb of that hand skyward. Imagine that you have a chain securely in your hand. The chain is five feet long and connected into a wall

Pull-the-chain drill. Several top tour players have loved this thought. It's great for feeling a strong lead side. Imagine a chain hooked into a wall. You have one chance to pull it free from this golf position. Keep the lead arm connected. The core, hips, and legs do the work, not the arm.

off your right side. You are holding the chain with very little slack. I'm giving you just one chance to pull the chain out of the wall. You wouldn't try to jerk the chain out with just the arm, would you? Instead, you would keep your arm connected to your body and use your entire body to pull the chain free. This is how you use the big muscles and core to multiply your power in the golf swing. See the illustration.

### Pro Example: Bryson DeChambeau

Doing it your way! I've loved my talks and discussions with Bryson. He's given tremendous thought to each piece of his swing. Here's a modern player who fully believes in breaking the golf swing into sections or steps to make the swing more repeatable and free in competition. Bryson also loves the analytics of the game. My first talk happened with Bryson when he was playing in the South Beach International Amateur over the Christmas season in Miami. I was the cochairman that year, and Bryson drove over at Doral to see me and for a chat. He knew I had spent a lot of time with Ben Doyle and that I was familiar with Homer Kelley's *The Golfing Machine*. I was so interested in his different approach to *The Golfing Machine*, which was the central part of our talk.

His swing did not resemble any of the swings I had seen taught by golfing machine teachers. Bryson was very aware of this observation. One issue I had with *The Golfing Machine* was the way it was being taught as a strict method. Since I had the opportunity to spend an entire afternoon with its author, Homer Kelly, at his home including five hours in his garage with all his training devices, I knew the idea of the book was that there were literally millions of ways to swing a golf club and not one way to teach the swing.

Homer thought a golfer should adhere to using fundamentals that lined up in the different swing models. The components were supposed to line up with acceptable variations. (But it was supercomplicated and tough to read.)

Instead, I had observed that every golfing machine instructor taught almost every aspect or section of the swing exactly the same way as Ben Doyle (who brought the golfing machine ideas to the world from Seattle, where he studied directly with Homer Kelly). From a book that was supposed to be an encyclopedia of different ways to swing, the instruction had mostly morphed into a one-way teaching method. I worked with Ben Doyle extensively. I watched carefully how he taught and how he spoke. Ben was one of the most prolific teachers in golf history. I know many other golfing machine teachers and saw that they wanted the left arm to be placed at 45 degrees at Step 3 with every student. I continued to keep my friendship with Ben until he died. I even had him do schools and lessons at my Texas facility. I always learned something from Ben, who was one of the most dedicated teachers in history.

By then, I had done decades of work on the JMGS system and I had been sure to leave out numerous problems I saw in that book and other methods. My idea has been to bring a unified teaching approach to the golf world based on top ball-strikers.

My dad was sure the *The Golfing Machine* was incomprehensible to almost every golfer. He was not certain about the validity of each part of the book, either. But my father could explain the book to me. Certainly that book, and my friendship with Ben Doyle, piqued my interest in breaking a golf swing down. My dad and I talked about segments of the golf swing. The system I developed for my golf schools is different from *The Golfing Machine* in many ways, but one difference was I used tour models for research, and I used safety zones. I knew there had to be parameters in teaching segments of the swing. I knew a tightly mandated golf method would not work for the vast majority of golfers.

Bryson modified his takeaway with the driver and long irons much differently. It's a no-hands, one-piece takeaway, meaning no wrist set at all. That's a huge departure from the well-known

*Bryson DeChambeau showing excellent footwork at Step 7c.*

**BUILD YOUR SWING**

golfing machine teachers, who all taught an early set of the wrists. Bryson went exactly the opposite way. There's nothing wrong with an early wrist set, but it's very different from what Bryson is doing and he's using the same book. I just find that so interesting. It is clear to me that you have to match up the entire style of your students. It means you should not teach every student the same way. I teach my staff to look at each player individually within our teaching system, using all of our teaching tools. Watch everything about them. Notice how they move. How fast do they talk? It might be something small, or something very obvious. Bryson is a big guy, he's strong, and he has a very upright swing motion. He's obviously more comfortable with moving everything away together in the backswing. That means slow. An early set moves things faster, which is exactly what Bryson does not want. My point here is that Bryson has gone totally in his own direction with a top teacher. He has a teacher he believes in, and they have a plan to follow. He's also very much into the physics and biomechanics of the golf swing. He continues to upgrade any part of his swing by continuously learning. Not many golf teachers can keep up with his vocabulary.

Something most golfers don't know about Bryson is his father was a golf professional and a really good player. How much influence did that have on a young Bryson DeChambeau? Hard to say, but it's another example of a top tour player having a top golf swing model during the imitative years. The lesson: work with a top instructor, but you can do things your own way. There is no single way for everybody.

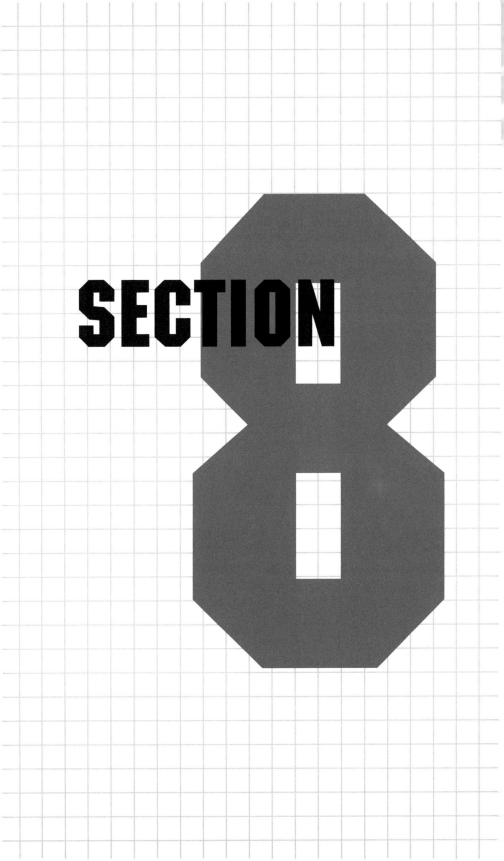

SECTION 8

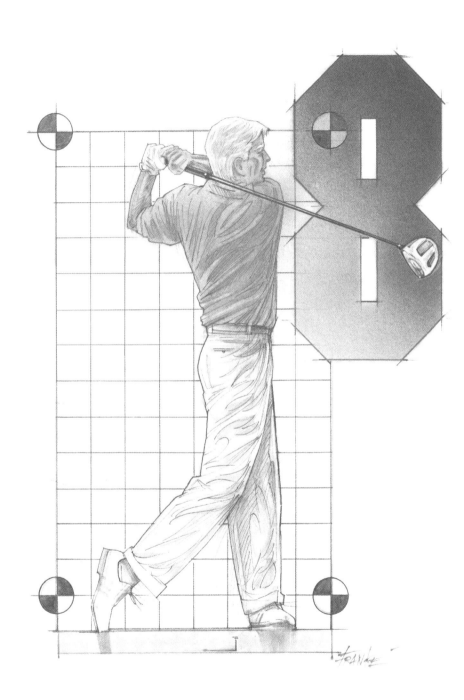

STEP 8

# STEP 8

# THE FINISH

"Point the club at the target in your backswing, finish with the shaft on your neck, and you will be a decent player." That simple logic comes from Jackie Burke, the former Masters and PGA champion. As a teacher to many of golf's greatest players, Jackie always had an interesting way of describing facets of the swing, and that quote is one of my favorites.

It sticks with students. It's one of those concepts that's hard to forget. The idea is pedagogical, meaning the teacher gives ideas from their experience that have actually produced success. All the great teachers I've known have that skill. You teach in a language your student understands. "You have not taught if the student hasn't learned," John Wooden famously said.

Let's talk about the finish of the golf swing in detail. I'll also describe how the club rebounds after the finish, another piece of the swing that can be underappreciated. This is the final step in the positions I teach. You can never be too good to ignore working on the finish. It's a fantastic position to focus on in tournament golf.

## FINISH AND REBOUND

I've had great results working on a player's overall swing by just teaching the finish position. If I can put a golfer in a good position when the swing ends, I see improvements in the other positions. If you get in that textbook finish, guess what happens? Miraculously, other swing mistakes disappear! It's a great way to learn how to swing with better form. Call it reverse engineering.

The renowned English golf instructor Leslie King taught his students the finish segments first. In fact, his first six lessons with a new student were on the follow-through and how to get into a balanced finish. He included "the rebound," as I call it. That's the move after you finish. It's bringing the club down in front of the chest with the clubface square. Although this seems so easy and natural to do for the advanced golfer, it must be taught precisely to the beginner or casual golfer.

The perfect finish.

## DOWN THE LINE

Ken Venturi was a big believer in finishing with the shaft angled through the ears. That's the classic full finish of so many great ball-strikers. The wrists have to be angled correctly, so the arms go to a relaxed position and the ball soars toward the target. This is a concept I've taught my students with great success. I like the shaft appearing to go through the ears or resting on the neck like you might see in the swings of the great Ernie Els, Rory McIlroy, Justin Thomas, or Jon Rahm.

Other things to check:

1. You're up on the right toe.
2. Your weight is balanced fully forward.
3. The right foot is just a prop.
4. Your body is tall.
5. You have rebounded the club correctly.

## THE REBOUND

After the completion of the swing, an expert golfer naturally rebounds the club back in front of the body. I have to teach this reflex action to most students who do not finish properly.

When you bring the club back, you should be watching ball flight and evaluating your shot. Your body is relaxed, and the tension is removed from your back muscles. All pressure in the hands dissipates. Tiger Woods was famous for letting the shaft slide down his hands and then spinning it after nailing a shot. Tiger's rebound is one of the most copied parts of his golf swing. I see juniors practicing spinning the shaft down just like him or Justin Thomas. I want you to get in the habit of thinking *finish and rebound,* and your consistency will improve.

## Pro Example: Rory McIlroy

I can't think of another golfer who finishes the swing and holds that textbook position better than Rory McIlroy. I first watched Rory play when he was only nine. He was at the Publix Junior Classic, an international tournament held each year at Doral. Rory was paired with my son, Jon, who now runs my golf schools. Jon went on to become an All-American junior and played college golf at Oklahoma State, where he lived with Rickie Fowler and Kevin Tway.

They were the top-ranked college team in the country. Rory McIlroy went on to become the No. 1 player in the world and a multiple major championship winner. I was very impressed with Rory way back then and remember telling that to his father, Jerry. In fact, Jerry and I reminisce about that day when our sons played together. I suggested he hook up with a teacher back in Ireland. Jerry arranged that, and Rory just continued to improve. He had that same great finish position he has now.

One of the very best swing thoughts is, "go to a complete and balanced finish." I know golfers have unique swing characteristics and no one looks the same. But there is one exception: all golfers should finish with their hips level, the clubshaft resting on the neck, and their weight fully supported by the lead leg. Done right, it's a beautiful thing to see.

I know that the simple thought of "get to a great finish" makes mistakes disappear. Small swing errors are suddenly corrected. I can't tell you how many times I've instructed my students to focus on the finish, and then later they come back and tell me they just played their best golf. I always ask my students to relax the shoulders, arms, and wrists at the finish, just like Rory looks in the illustration and photos.

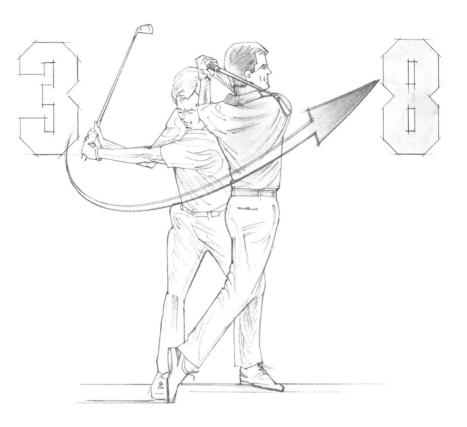

A great way to practice a pro finish. Take a three-quarter swing to Position 3. Get the club in good slot position (shaft near 45 degrees). Stay smooth. Now swing to the pro finish at 70 percent effort. I'd advise using a tee.

Here are a few things it will automatically improve:

1. Your swing tempo gets better.
2. Your sequence improves.
3. Your rotation through the shot is better.
4. Your grip pressure is more relaxed from start to finish.

## MORE ON THE REBOUND

After a better golfer finishes the swing, typically there's a reflex action. The golfer brings the arms back down in front of the body and the back muscles are relaxed.

I've learned that this rebound movement helps my students complete the swing properly. I have them bring the arms down with their elbows reasonably close to each other. I also ask them to relax the body. It's a tremendous teaching tool and helps everyone. They all improve with this pro trick. Here's your mantra: *Go to a full finish. Rebound the club. Evaluate the shot.*

### Key Ideas

1. In this final phase of the swing, I hope that momentum guides you into the same finish position as an accomplished golfer. When that happens, you've really felt a true swinging motion. One feeling can be to have the swing of the arms and club pull you into a good finish. Often, the high-handicap golfer turns the shoulders ahead of the club's swing. They spin out and swing over the plane. When you get out in front of the swing, you'll never achieve that beautifully balanced finish.

2. Your right shoulder should be closer to the target than your left shoulder.

3. A fundamental of top ball-strikers is that they will have some spine tilt toward the target at the finish. Remember this.

-LEXI THOMPSON
AT FINISH!

Notice the slight tilt of her body toward the target line. Her eyes are up. Head rotated to watch the flight of the ball. Clubshaft is through the ears.

**THE FINISH**

Practice trying to finish with your spine tilted slightly toward the target line, not perfectly vertical.

Jordan Spieth finishing with the shaft on the neck.

### Finish Keys

When you complete the pro finish and rebound the club to evaluate your shot, three important items have been achieved:

1. Optimum balance.
2. Optimum feedback.
3. Optimum feel.

## DRILLS

### Pocket Drill

Place an alignment rod or a golf shaft on the ground. Without holding a club, take your stance with the shaft in between your feet. Put your hands on each hip or into your pockets—one on the left side of the shaft and the other on the right. The goal here is to mimic a swing and finish with the trail hand/pocket in front of the shaft. That pocket replaces the position of the front pocket. When you turn through the shot, the lead hip rotates, and the trail hip fires forward. Squeeze your glutes as you finish the swing. Stretch upwards to a tall finish. Replace the lead pocket with the trail pocket.

## Grip-Pressure Check at the Finish

I ask my students to check how hard they're holding the club when they finish. I like them to feel the same amount of pressure they had in their hands when holding the club at address.

Many golfers tense up through impact and are gripping the club way too tight when they finish. Others loosen their hands as the swing ends, which is another bad habit. When you practice, pay close attention to your grip pressure. Use my grip scale to establish the right amount of pressure and maintain it throughout the swing. Four is a good number on a scale from 1 to 10.

## Mirror Drill

I think using a mirror is one of the very best ways to practice getting into a pro finish. Swing the club and hold your finish. Check it in the mirror from all angles and adjust it, if necessary, to make it look great. Watch pros you like and how they finish and try to copy them. Keep rehearsing, and soon it will help your entire swing.

## INTERESTING REBOUNDS

There have been many unique rebounds, and some have become signature moves. Tiger has a rebound where he whips the club down violently off his neck. When Tiger smashes a drive, the shaft literally bounces off his neck and rebounds back in front of his body. I've actually taught this to my top junior golfers to increase confidence and speed during their golf swings.

I also loved Johnny Miller's rebound. He would bring the club down in front of his face, pointing the shaft in line with his target. That way, he could trace the flight of his shots. His longtime caddie, Andy Martinez, told me Johnny wanted to see his ball fly dead straight and stay on line with the flagstick from impact to landing. I don't think anyone has ever hit better iron shots than Johnny Miller did for a period of about ten years.

Lee Trevino loved to fade the ball and would rebound his clubshaft in a fade orientation leaning to the right. Tons of tour players have copied Lee's signature rebound. Johnny Miller did to hit his fade shots. There are many others, but hopefully these give you a sense of the importance of the rebound. Come up with your own signature move.

## APPENDIX

# SOME FINAL THOUGHTS

## MCLEAN ROTATIONS AND SWING-PLANE FUNDAMENTALS:

1. The shoulders turn on an axis.
2. The hips turn on an axis.
3. The clubhead moves on an arc.
4. The shaft moves along an inclined plane.

I'm with my teaching staff and visually explaining the X-Factor coil to Grayson Zacker, Joe Compitello, Bobby Cole, and Glen Farnsworth. All are lead master instructors.

229

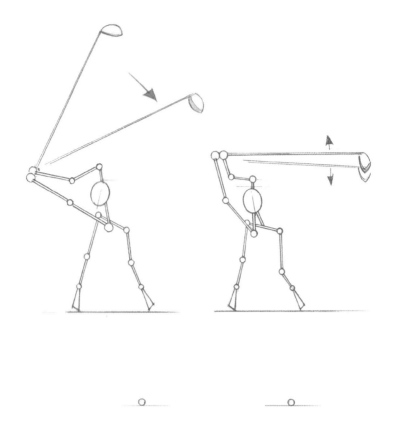

Looking closely at joints and rotations. The work done behind the scenes for top teaching.

I've seen and read about instructors advocating a level hip turn, but that is incorrect because you bend forward from the hip joints, and your pelvis has a forward tilt. We measured it to be approximately 5 to 9 degrees of tilt. Shorter golfers have less forward tilt than taller ones.

## ROTATIONS

As the rib cage and shoulders rotate, so does the pelvis. You can see the rotations are on an inclined plane in the above illustration. The pelvis turns on the flattest plane, but it's not level. Level is particularly damaging if you rotate the lead hip level with the ground in the downswing—it's the classic slicer's move. From the face-on angle, the lead hip must move laterally and vertically up through impact. I've had many high-handicap golfers twist their hips level like a merry-go-round, and that led to a violent, over-the-top, steep downswing.

My top amateur student of all time, George Zahringer, prefers to rotate the rib cage to gain a bigger shoulder turn. That's another way to feel proper shoulder rotation. The idea of turning the rib cage should be done on an angled turn, so that the right shoulder elevates in your coil.

## THE HIPS TURN ON AN AXIS

### Down-the-line Drill for Hip Action

Grab a club and get into your setup with your hip pockets pressed lightly against a wall. Now make a backswing keeping your right hip touching the wall. As you start the forward swing, also stay against the wall with the right hip. The left pocket should also be against the wall as you simulate the impact position. In fact, that pocket stays against the wall to Step 7a before finally coming off the wall at Step 8. It's a great drill to stop onward extension.

## USING YOUR LIMITED PRACTICE TIME

By the time I took the director of golf position at Sleepy Hollow Country Club in New York, I had given thousands of lessons. I was working with many of the top amateurs in the New York City area and many PGA and LPGA players. Soon I would be one of the first teachers to help start the Golf Channel. I also helped my two sons by coaching their baseball and basketball teams, not to mention their golf games.

My time practicing golf was very limited, and I'm sure it's like that for many of you reading this book. Yet I played some of my best golf during those super hectic years. In 1993, I shot every round in the sixties for an entire summer playing with the members at Sleepy Hollow. We had a yearlong, pro-am event where I played with a different group of members every weekend. I also finished in the top ten of every PGA section event that year.

The point is, even if you have only a very limited amount of time, you can improve if you use that time effectively. The advice in this book will help a great deal. You will get better if you follow the steps I've outlined. Focus on the section or sections of your swing that need correction. Then practice diligently anywhere you can, even in your home. So much can be accomplished simply by improving your practice swing. I can't emphasize enough how important it is to make good golf moves. That's how I teach my students. That's what I've done best—help students understand where they need to be at each of the twelve steps in the swing, and how to practice those steps to make the overall movement a lot better. If you know a section of your swing is poor, then practice doing it correctly in small movements. Repeat the correct motions over and over, and you will improve—promise.

Here are my suggestions for how to get the most out of your practice:

1. **Work on the start and finish.** Get in front of a mirror for a couple of minutes every day, and work on your setup and your finish. Even one minute doing each will make a difference.
2. **Rehearse impact alignments.** The hands must lead the clubhead into impact. Visualize to make that happen. Whenever you practice or have time to swing the club, simulate impact with your head behind the ball and the shaft leaning slightly forward.

3. Get help from a qualified instructor. As a well-known teacher, even I needed help or a pair of eyes on me before competition. I worked with a teacher before I played in any tournament. Dave Collins was my guy. I would practice my positions with Dave in slow motion. We'd go over my preshot routine and hit shots at specific targets with tempo and rhythm. We discussed the tournament venue. I would then go out with Dave on the course the night before the event. We might play only a handful of holes, but I was accountable for every shot, having to describe what I wanted the ball to do before I hit it. I'd then swing and hold my finish position every time.

4. Don't ignore short putting. Almost every single day, I did the exact same routine on the putting green. I allotted twenty minutes for it and set my watch. I used a putting training aid for fifteen minutes and then putted for five minutes without it, trying to roll the ball in from short distances up to seven feet. This book is just about swing mechanics and technique, but it should be obvious that putting matters.

5. Take care of your body. When you go to the range always warm up with a few stretches before you hit shots. Focus on the lower back and the hips. One stretch I like is to put a club over your shoulders. Then whirl the club with the wrists and arms. Practice your backswing and through-swing motions, making sure you stay in the proper forward tilt. If the sun is out, watch your shadow to monitor if your head is swaying or drifting. Most golfers I see at the range do golf exercises poorly. Please try hard to make good practice swings.

6. Have a range routine. Jack Nicklaus and Tiger Woods practiced by starting with short wedges, then moving

233

through the clubs in their bags in this order: full wedges, 8 iron, 4 iron, 3 wood, and driver. They ended with a few more easy wedges and then headed to the putting green. I'm not saying it's the best way to warm up, but it sure worked for two of golf's greatest players. You need to establish your own routine. Many tour players use alignment rods every time they practice. Others like to putt first and then do the range work.

7. Always remember that tension kills the golf swing! During the busiest time of my life, I worked as the director of golf at Sleepy Hollow half the year and then ran my golf school at the Doral Resort the other half. (I did that for two years.) I shot 63 in a Met PGA professional event and finished second in the Met PGA Championship. (I also shot a 27 for nine holes in that PGA event.) By using my very limited time to practice in a very organized way like I'm suggesting you do, I kept my game at a high level. I could go play with my tour professional students and hit all the shots. The ideas I employed to maximize practice time worked, and I've since shared them with others who have busy lives and limited time to practice.

## THE IDEA OF TEACHING THE PERFECT SWING

### My Version of the Perfect Swing

The easiest thing to teach is perfect positions with no safety zones. I say this for many reasons, but mostly because you teach the same details to every student. When I collaborated with engineers and scientists in Toronto to develop one of the first high-definition golf simulators (HD Golf), I showed them the theoretical perfect-swing positioning of the club and body.

To do that, I used the geometry of the perfect swing plane and the ideal body positions to achieve it. I used an inclined plane for the shaft-plane alignment at impact. With the help of the scientists, we modeled a theoretical perfect swing.

Placing the club perfectly in the backswing is easy to demonstrate. You show them exactly where you think the wrists should be positioned. The club is held with a classic grip, the shaft points through the belt buckle, and the clubface is set square. At halfway back, the model has put the club parallel to the target line and parallel to the spine. At Step 3, the shaft points directly at the target line, perfectly on plane with a square clubface. At the top of the backswing, the club's shaft should point directly down the target line with the clubface square. This is a perfect Step 4 position!

Transition starts while the club is still traveling back, and the lower body moves forward. The shaft moves on the perfect plane with tremendous speed. They strike the dead center of the clubface. The clubhead exits perfectly up the inclined plane of the shaft. The golfer flows to a balanced finish position and rebounds the club. There is tremendous power but with an effortless look. Everything is in this swing is perfect—tempo, timing, rhythm, and path.

## Backswing

A perfect backswing is something almost anybody could physically learn within a month of diligent practice. Jackie Burke told me that forty-five years ago. He also said to "check the position of the top five players each year." You'll find five different positions. Jackie told me that it's not a perfect backswing that creates great shots or great players. As you have read in this book, the moment of truth happens in transition. I'm not saying a beautiful backswing is not a very good thing. I'm saying the safety zones for the backswing arm and shaft positions are fairly liberal and not the same for all great ball-strikers (past or present). The corridors of success provide room for individuality.

The backswings of all the great ball-strikers look different. To name several: Ben Hogan, Sam Snead, Arnold Palmer, Jack Nicklaus, Lee Trevino, Nick Faldo, Greg Norman, Hideki Matsuyama, Tiger Woods, Rory McIlroy, Freddie Couples, Dustin Johnson, Justin Thomas, Jon Rahm, Bryson DeChambeau, Gary Woodland, and Tony Finau. The clubface or clubshaft and arm angles are in a different position for each of them at Step 4. But when you look closely and examine their body positions, you will see more similarities and you will see great transition. The timing will follow the kinematic sequence for power and accuracy.

## Differences at Setup

Start with body alignments at setup. We see differences with different clubs. Each player has his or her unique structure. These players set up to suit their body shape or the intended shot shape.

When you get right down to it, you adjust for wind, slope, and how you're hitting the ball that particular day. I've said it thousands of times: "Golf is a game of adjustments."

The fictional character Shivas Irons was quoted in the book *Golf in the Kingdom* as saying, "You will never make the same swing for the rest of your life." I never forgot that line. It's a good one, and I think it might be true. Top players come close to replicating their swing, but every shot is likely slightly different. Go with your favorite shot every time.

## FORCE PLATES AND MOTION

When I look at the most advanced force plates, or pressure mats, on the most sophisticated measuring devices, it's obvious that the top players move pressure (or weight) slightly differently. No pressure map of a tour player looks exactly the same, which goes right to my premise that all swings are different. At my schools, we believe that every golfer has their own swing. We teach great moves, great club angles, great swing plane, and great positions, but we adapt to our players. Using BodiTrak, we check pressure distribution and can see accurately if it's toward the toes or heels. We can measure how effectively the student loads and transitions, but we also can identify death moves very quickly. That's the greatest benefit of force plates.

There are definite death moves in the motion of poor golfers. However, I know from teaching world-class players that they all have their own signature. A good teacher must know what not to change.


## MASTERY

I know I've had an advantage over most other teachers, because I've been exposed to much more great golf for many more years. First as a player, and then being onsite for decades of tour golf. Believe me, I put in the time too. I've been obsessed with learning everything about the game. My advantage was playing often with PGA TOUR players, spending huge chunks of time with the best teachers, and also being in the right place at the right time.

Now there is modern biomechanics and phenomenal technical information, so it's much easier to learn how golf swings should work. It's interesting to point out that biomechanics really proved ideas that Carl Welty, my teaching teams, and already knew from our research. I like that the biomechanics team tested ideas and proved them. They might explain the ideas in engineering terms or in anatomically correct language, and that's better than I did with *The X-Factor Swing* and other books and articles I've written.

But you can't learn to teach golf quickly—at least not well. The danger in teaching is not giving enough technical information but rather making golf too impossible to learn. Any top teacher has to work with all types of players and put in real time on the range. You have to do the time, learn from the best, and have a plan. A top teacher gets the students better consistently. The vocabulary used must be understandable. The smartest people like Albert Einstein and Steve Jobs have spoken and written about the beauty of simplicity.

## Pedagogy

Pedagogy is the ability to teach at a master level, having many ways to say or illustrate an idea, knowing that one of those ways will be absorbed better than the others from student to student. This is a word that is used to describe a truly great teacher who is doing little things that might go unnoticed by most. In truth, you have not taught until the student learns. Simply having knowledge and advanced vocabulary does not mean you can teach students and have them improve every time.

Since there are 7.5 billion people on this planet and every person is unique, teaching one model will never work for any sport. The teacher has to adapt to the student, not the other way around. It's also the main reason my teachers have learned to teach differently for the beginner or infrequent golfer. We focus much more on the small muscles for the level one golfer, learning from the green outward. The average mid-handicap golfer (level two) must learn the inside attack to the ball and a good introduction to weight transfer and good footwork. The advanced player (level three) will be syncing up the powerful body movements with slotting the club repeatedly. The advanced player will be controlling the clubface with minimal conscious effort.

## Position Teaching and Building Blocks and Steps

There are twelve key teaching positions or building blocks in my golf swing system. JMGS instructors must learn them cold to be certified to teach at my golf schools. You can learn them in this book and use them to diagnose your own swing. These positions are the building blocks for your golf swing. My staff and I analyze every swing this way to find and correct the problems preventing someone from hitting quality shots. I've been instructing like this for forty years, and the results of position teaching speak for themselves. It is—by far—the best way to learn how to swing a golf club. No matter your skill, you can improve your ball-striking if you use the ideas presented in this book.

In a building-block approach you start from the beginning—first things first!

The key concepts to my formula:

1. Have a procedure.
2. Do things in a logical order.
3. Use a flexible system, so you can teach golfers of every level, size, and shape.
4. Know that every person you teach is an individual.
5. Use pictures, video, or in-person demonstrations to aid in the learning process.

The view from above, checking shoulder positions and rotations.

## Golf Swing Instruction

This book delves deeply into ball-striking, which is just one segment of JMGS teaching program. I covered other areas in *The Eight-Step Swing*. The centerpiece of JMGS is the 25 Percent Theory, which divides golf into four equal parts—the long game, the short game, the mental game, and the management game.

I learned my system by playing alongside and gleaning information from the very best players and then by studying great teachers. I watched, listened, and studied their ideas on every aspect of golf. I watched how the best instructors taught the swing. I also studied coaches in other pro sports. Through these

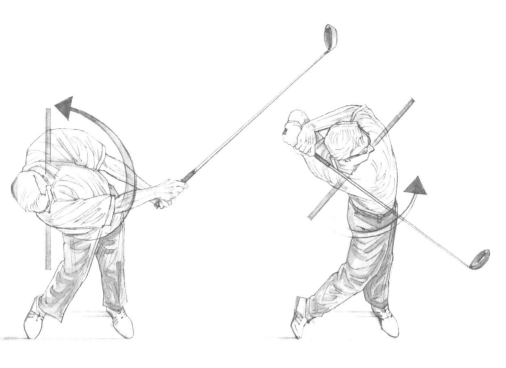

experiences, I confirmed that all top businesspeople and top coaches use a system.

Every golfer needs solid ideas to rely upon. We all need fundamentals to fall back on whenever the swing is off. Then you will know the path back to your ball-striking success.

Golf will always be a game of adjustments.

## Criticism of Position Teaching

When I wrote *The Eight-Step Swing*, some criticized the concept of using positions to teach the overall golf swing. That book was not the first to focus on position teaching, but since I was able to explain it on the Golf Channel, it received tremendous attention. Critics said the swing should be taught as one continuous motion and not in a step-by-step learning process. I don't hear that criticism anymore. Golf students know my system works, as do the other top teachers in the game. Numerous instructors have taken key components from my position teaching and incorporated them into their writing and method of teaching. There is no great golf teacher who does not teach positions to his or her students!

## The Difference in a System

To be clear, my system does not mandate perfect positions. This is what separates the system from other approaches to golf instruction and methods of teaching.

I teach positions, but there are "safety zones" within each segment. As long as my golfers can approximate the position I'm advocating—think of it as corridor of success—then their swings improve. I'm not asking you to swing like a robot, and I'm not trying to mold each of my students into one model. I'm sure that's why we are so good at coaching all levels of golfers.

All top coaches break down their sport into essential components. Business executives do the same. Doctors do the same. This is how you achieve your goals. I think you'll be pleasantly surprised how easy it is to remember each of the twelve steps in this book, and you can learn them as fast or as slowly as you want. The photos and illustrations in this book will bring the words and instruction to life. You'll likely discover you can keep many individual characteristics your swing already possesses. In short, you can build a good golf swing and own new positions through repetition. Do the practice movements correctly and you will improve.

As Henry Ford put it, "Nothing is particularly hard if you divide into small jobs."

242

# CONCLUSION

Thery are many ways to play great golf and hit great shots. The range of teaching ideas runs from the extreme-thrower style instruction of Ernest Jones, to the extreme-dragger style instruction exemplified by most golfing machine teachers.

There are obviously different models for success. However, there are definitely rules you must learn and incorporate into your golf swing to gain improvement. You just cannot hit consistent golf shots from bad positions. Remember, sometimes a student needs more release and sometimes more lag and drag.

When I started teaching this way, I found success with any level golfer virtually every time. Developing the JM System was important for me when I developed my golf schools. After going through my training manuals, video presentations, and attending our training meetings, all of my teachers could easily adapt to my system. I knew I needed a comprehensive and universal system that could teach students of every level from beginners to major champions. My teachers also needed the freedom to express their own ideas and concepts, within the safety zones or the corridors of success in the system I developed. The better the teacher can play good golf, the easier it is for him or her to adapt quickly to teaching within the safety zones. But they all must know the fundamentals in this book.

243

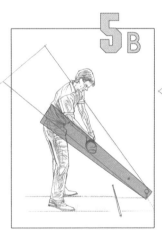

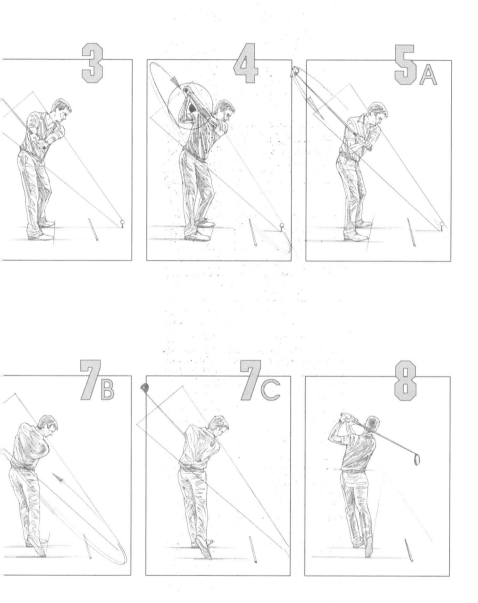

CONCLUSION

We all need creative powers to be special at our profession. My certified teachers are free to use their own genius. All of my teachers know that swing positions that fall outside of the safety zones should be changed. The concept I have used for movements outside the safety zones is "death positions."

This book is the ultimate building-block approach for developing a functional golf swing, no matter your age, weight, height, arm length, or physical limitations. We are all different, with different levels of nerves, tension, visual perception, and athleticism.

As one of golf's greatest players and teachers famously said to me when I was at the University of Houston, "If all you had to do to hit great golf shots was to take the club to a square position and point it down the target line at the top, everyone would be great." He followed that line with "How stupid could you be, McLean?"

That was said by the great Jackie Burke, who has been so important in how I developed my business and many ideas on the golf swing.

The twelve building blocks, or twelve steps, are great teaching positions, but with the safety zones clearly marked out. Remember that the swings of the greatest players, current and all-time, all look a little different—especially at the top of the backswing. But they are all swinging within the safety zones. This is absolutely true for the critical positions starting in the downswing to halfway through the finish.

I know the great illustrations and photographs make this book easy to follow. Great pictures make learning so much easier. I covered many details on how I teach in a building- block fashion. You might need to read some of the sections several times. But I can guarantee you that learning the golf swing through positions is the fastest and best way to develop your swing.

Come see me at one of my golf schools!

# AUTHOR'S NOTE

I have never taught all twelve segments to any student during one lesson. These are checkpoint positions I use with video to accurately diagnose and fix golf swings. If you are studying your swing on video, what would you study? How would you know what to look for or what to check? Where would you stop the video?

This book provides the answers. After decades of detailed research, the safety zones are here for you to understand.

## ACHIEVING EFFORTLESS POWER

To swing the club smooth and with tempo, timing, and rhythm, you need a swing that allows you to hit shots with fluidity. Great tempo, rhythm, and timing is what you see in the swings of top amateurs and pro golfers. When you are out of position, you will always look awkward and out of balance. Position teaching begins at setup and ends with a beautiful finish.

You can now understand what works in a golf swing and what will never work. I'm a first-things-first teacher, so I recommend starting at setup. Then check your swing to see where you might go wrong. The positions show you how to accurately determine

247

and fix mistakes. Understanding the dynamics of a swing allows you to stop your golf swing on video and make improvements. Use the concepts and drills shown in each section to make the necessary changes.

# ACKNOWLEDGMENTS

This book is a detailed follow up on *The Eight-Step Swing*, only this book focuses exclusively on the golf swing and the twelve sections of the swing. These sections—or steps, or checkpoints, or building blocks—are used every day at my golf schools. I know the golf knowledge of the average amateur has increased tremendously. Therefore, it is time to produce this more comprehensive JMGS book on position teaching. We have proved that the step-by-step building block approach is the best way to learn and teach the swing. I thank the more than four hundred teachers who have gone through the intensive training at JMGS. I am proud of their continued success and grateful for all the input they provided for teaching golf to beginners, intermediate, and advanced golf students. I also thank the many tour players I've worked with for the opportunity to teach the best in the world and learn so much walking the tour fairways. I've also been fortunate to work with many of the most-recognized teachers on the planet. Many of these teachers became good friends, or we have done major teaching seminars together.

Phil Franké did the fantastic illustrations and poured his heart into this project. I must have driven him crazy with details, but Phil never complained. The visuals are so important to understanding the written word. I think we have accomplished this aspect. Matt Rudy did great work on the first year of writing, and then I decided to focus solely on the golf swing. Matt was so good to work with and I thank him very much. Ron Kapriske, also from *Golf Digest*, did my final editing. Ron cleaned the dialogue and took out repeat information. Ron has a great appreciation for the mechanics of the golf swing and is a top writer for *Golf Digest*. Thanks Ron. My friend and top teacher, Joe Compitello, took the photographs. Mark Fretz at Radius Book Group stayed after me through this three-year project. I thank him for hanging with me when I was almost ready to throw in the towel. I probably came close to driving him crazy too. Dita Spencer, my executive assistant (at our headquarters in Miami) typed out hundreds of pages and rewrote them.

While I was writing this book, Carl Welty passed away. Carl Welty was the most important teacher in my life. We formed a partnership on golf research. Carl was a golf research scientist and he insisted on doing all of our filming in a precise way. Then, we could compare tour swings from perfect angles. He was maniacal about being precise.

The knowledge I gained from Carl shows up in many places. He was a great friend and together we studied golf swings in a super detailed fashion few would ever believe. He was the best golf swing researcher in the world. The knowledge we gained together came through in *The Eight-Step Swing* book and has been used by many teachers (in their writings or other publications).

The research comes with the help of Carl, or my staff of teachers. I spent thousands of hours to discover and understand how to teach all levels of golfers. Knowledge eventually appears from many different sources and we all benefit. I'm glad I've had a hand in moving modern teaching forward. I hope this book also contributes to the knowledge base of golfers and teachers everywhere.

I have to mention a few special mentors.

I met Jackie Burke (Masters champion, PGA champion, leading money winner on the PGA TOUR, six Ryder Cups, PGA Hall of Fame) as a freshman at the University of Houston and developed a lifelong friendship. Jackie was like a second father to me. We did golf schools at my clubs in New York and later at PGA West and Doral. Jackie Burke is a gift to my career. He and three-time Masters champion Jimmy Demaret built the famous Champions Golf Club in Houston, Texas, where Jackie ran everything. Both were close friends with Ben Hogan who came to Houston each year and stayed at the Champions.

Al Mengert had worked for Claude Harmon at Winged Foot in New York. Al played the PGA TOUR and later moved to Tacoma, Washington, near my home. My first professional lessons were with him. Al told me so many stories about New York and teaching in that part of America. Al also worked under the great Tommy Armour. It's a big reason I chose to start my professional life in New York.

I met Ken Venturi (U.S. Open champion) in 1975. We developed a close relationship. I worked very hard on my own game with him and later with him on the teaching side of golf. Ken was a great friend to me for thirty years. Ken Venturi was also the lead analyst at CBS golf telecasts. He was on top of everything on the PGA TOUR. Ken passed away in 2011 and I was a pallbearer at his funeral.

The Harmon family: I spent many hours with Claude Harmon at Winged Foot and then in Rancho Mirage, California, when I was the director of golf and the head professional at Tamarisk Country Club. Claude was across the street at Morningside and had taught golf for fifty years. He was an innovator in camera research for golf. I loved talking to him about Hogan, about other greats, and teaching in general. His sons were all my friends; Dick Harmon was head professional at River Oaks

Country Club. Dick and I did many PGA workshops and seminars together. Dick helped me set up the Met PGA section junior golf program. One time, Dick brought his brother Butch to do a workshop in Houston with us, which was fuel that helped Butch to become a top teacher. Since that time, we developed a close relationship too. Craig Harmon was the pro at the famous Oak Hill Golf Club and also a tremendous teacher. Billy Harmon is my age and we have been friends forever. All the Harmon boys are great teachers.

My golf library at home contains over fifteen hundred golf books, all of which I have read. I have been obsessed with learning and I feel like I almost know some of those old writers. Many of my books have been signed by the player or the teacher, many of them people I knew well.

My mother and father were good golfers. My dad qualified for three U.S. Senior Amateurs and won numerous club championships. He maintained a zero handicap for decades. He was my first teacher and my mom was the one who took me everywhere to tournaments all over the Pacific Northwest.

Getting to know coach John Wooden (ten NCAA championships) was another blessing. Spending time with him at his Westwood condo and calling him at home, I learned so much about practice concepts and motivating players.

I've spent huge chunks of time with many great teachers around the world doing seminars, workshops, or coaching summits. I learned something from all of them. I've had over 260 former teachers or assistants move into top positions at famous private clubs in America, and a few outside of America, including Charlie Briggs (director of golf and GM at Burning Tree in Washington, D.C.), Darrell Kestner (Deepdale, New York), Christopher Toulson (Sunningdale CC, Scarsdale, New York), Chad Middaugh (Muirfield Village CC, Ohio), Sean Golden (Plainfield CC, New Jersey), Adam Kolloff (Liberty National, New Jersey),

Michael Hunt (Bayonne GC, New Jersey), Rick Hartman (The Atlantic Club, Illinois), Jeff Warne (The Bridge CC, Bridgehamptons, NY), John Bierkan (Aronimink CC, Pennsylvania), Jon Paupore (Red Ledges CC, Utah), Jon Horner (Cordevalle CC, San Jose, California), Matt McLean (The Concession GC, Florida, and Fishers Island Club, New York), Bryan Lebedevitch (PGA West, California), Kevin Sprecher (Sleepy Hollow CC, Scarborough-on-Hudson, New York), Jon McLean (The Club at 3 Creek, Jackson Hole, Wyoming), Sam Wiley (Wee Burn CC, Connecticut), Brett Bridgeman (Singapore CC, Singapore), Eric Lillibridge (Casa de Campo, Dominican Republic), and way too many others to list. They are incredible professionals.